CAPITAL AND OPERATING LEASES

A RESEARCH REPORT

Prepared by

Susan S. K. Lee

Federal Accounting Standards Advisory Board

October 2003

NOTE: This report was prepared by Ms. Susan S. K. Lee, Special Assistant at the Federal Aviation Administration while on assignment with FASAB. This material is presented for discussion purposes only; it is not intended to reflect authoritative views of the FASAB or its Staff. Official positions of the FASAB are determined only after extensive due process and deliberations.

About the Author

SUSAN S. K. LEE

Susan Lee has worked at the Federal Aviation Administration since 1991, serving as the Special Assistant to the Chief Financial Officer and later the Special Projects Officer to the Director, Office of Financial Management. In these roles she has worked on both accounting and budget matters and represented the CFO and the Director of Financial Management in meetings and various task groups. Recently, Susan was the audit liaison for the financial statements audit and directed the preparation of FAA's *Performance and Accountability Report* and supplemental *Highlights* document.

Previous to the FAA, Susan worked at the National Archives and Records Administration as the agency's Director of Accounting and Director of Budget. She worked for the Treasury Department for 16 years, where she was the Director of the Federal Financial Systems Program, in charge of a staff who worked with the Office of Management and Budget (OMB) and the 23 largest Federal agencies to provide policy direction and to oversee agencies' progress in improving their financial systems. She served as Treasury's Fiscal Service representative on the Chief Financial Officers' Council, the CFO Subcommittee on Financial Systems and Information Needs, and the Systems Committee of the President's Council on Management Improvement. She also worked at the Office of Management and Budget for two years, during which she drafted OMB Bulletin No. 83-21, which was OMB's directive on using credit bureaus for debt collection, and led a government-wide task force to implement provisions of the Debt Collection Act.

An active supporter of the Association of Government Accountants (AGA), Susan has been the President of the Washington Chapter, National Treasurer, Regional Vice President, National Executive Committee member, and a permanent member of the AGA National Board of Directors. She was elected three times to be on the Board of Directors of the American Association of Budget and Program Analysis, and served as their Vice President for Membership and Vice president for Communications. She has been a member of the Brookings Institute Accountants' Roundtable and was Programs Chair for the Comptrollers' Roundtable. When AGA established the Certified Government Financial Manager (CGFM) designation, Susan was a subject matter expert who helped AGA to develop the knowledge requirements and the training materials used to prepare individuals for the professional examination. She graduated from the University of Maryland in 1976 and was a Certified Public Accountant from 1994 to 2002.

TABLE OF CONTENTS

CAPITAL AND OPERATING LEASES
RESEARCH PHASE

INTRODUCTION

Purpose and Objectives

The purpose of this research is to recommend whether or not additional FASAB guidance on leases is needed. Based on the project plan, (see Appendix No. 1), the objectives of the research are two-fold:

1. To develop a summary paper that permits staff and the Board to familiarize themselves with lease accounting under FASAB, FASB, GASB and international public sector accounting standards, and to familiarize them with global issues related to lease accounting, and

2. To aid in determining if new uses of leases by Federal entities create different and/or more urgent needs for FASAB guidance.

Scope

To accomplish these objectives, I reviewed existing standards, technical guidance, and issue papers on leases issued by FASAB, FASB, GASB, and the IFAC Public Sector Committee; reviewed OMB's guidance on scoring leases, [1] CBO's paper, *The Budgetary Treatment of Leases and Public/Private Ventures*, [2] GAO's report on *Alternative Approaches to Finance Federal Capital*,[3] and Treasury's U.S. Standard General Ledger (USSGL) and approved USSGL scenarios. Appendix No. 2 is a list of the available authoritative literature on leases.

Also reviewed were various reports and articles on lease issues and on a new approach for accounting for leases. To identify new uses of leases by federal entities, I reviewed GAO and CBO reports, Standards & Poor credit profiles, and news articles on specific lease agreements, including leases involving DOD, TVA, GSA, and Energy.

I spoke with representatives from Justice, Agriculture, OMB, GAO, DOD, GSA, FASB, GASB, and IFAC. Also meetings were held with Treasury to discuss the accounting logic for posting leases and with CBO to discuss the results of their research on public private partnerships. (See list of contacts in Appendix No. 3). I also attended a USSGL meeting to establish contacts and to seek preliminary information on how agencies' account for leases and how they disclose the use of leases in their financial statements.

---

[1] OMB Circular A-11, Preparation and Submission of Annual Budget Estimates, Appendix B. OMB also presents the requirements under which a lease-purchase or capital lease must be justified in Circular A-94, Guidelines and Discount Rates for Benefit-Cost Analysis of Federal Programs.
[2] A CBO Paper, The Budgetary Treatment of Leases and Public/Private Ventures, February 2003.
[3] GAO-03-1011, Budget Issues - Alternative Approaches to Finance Federal Capital, August 2003.

Background

Research on Federal lease accounting was initiated for several reasons. At the October 2002 meeting of the FASAB Board, the Office of Inspector General, Department of Justice, presented issues on accounting for leases and leasehold improvements that they wished to have addressed. Their specific concerns related to occupancy agreements between GSA and other Federal agencies, accounting for leasehold improvements, and the impact of a funding clause in a lease agreement.

During this era of funding constraints, renting under a lease contract, in lieu of purchasing an asset, has reemerged as a popular means for federal agencies to acquire the use of assets. From the vantage of an agency, an operating lease arrangement can be very attractive because the agency can acquire the use of an asset without having to secure appropriations for the entire cost of the asset up front. An operating lease spreads the cost of the asset over several years, albeit often at a higher cost to the Government.

There is proposed legislation expanding the authority of agencies to use leases as part of a program to improve agencies' management of assets. Also, increasingly, Congress has authorized specific agencies to enter into lease arrangements to obtain capital assets.

When FASAB issued its guidance on leases as part of SFFAS No. 5,[4] and SFFAS No. 6,[5] FASAB recognized that this was a topic that would require further study due to its complexity. FASAB staff regularly receives inquiries from agencies to clarify and interpret its lease guidance.

---

[4] SFFAS No. 5, Accounting for Liabilities of the Federal Government, December 20, 1995.
[5] SFFAS No. 6, Accounting for Property, Plant, and Equipment, November 30, 1995.

SUMMARY OF FASAB GUIDANCE
DIFFERENCE BETWEEN FASAB STANDARDS AND OTHER STANDARDS

What is a lease?

According to FASB, a lease is an agreement conveying the right to use property, plant, and equipment (PP&E) usually for a stated period of time. Specifically excluded are lease agreements to explore or exploit resources such as oil, gas, minerals, and timber, and licensing agreements for items like motion picture films, plays, manuscripts, patents, and copyrights. Likewise, IFAC defines a lease as an agreement whereby the lessor conveys to the lessee in return for a payment or series of payments the right to use an asset for an agreed period of time. IFAC, too, excludes lease agreements for natural resources and licensing agreements.

What is covered in FASAB guidance on leases?

FASAB guidance on leases is covered in SFFAS No. 5, *Accounting for Liabilities of the Federal Government*, (See Appendix No. 13) and SFFAS No. 6, *Accounting for Property, Plant, and Equipment* (See Appendix No. 14). Both standards define "capital lease" and list the four criteria used to determine whether or not a lease is a capital lease or an operating lease.

SFFAS No. 5 also discusses:

- The amount to be recorded by the lessee as a liability;
- The discount rate to be used; and
- The allocation of the payment between the obligation and interest expense.

Appendix B of SFFAS No. 5 provides an explanation of the expense and liability that should be recognized for a capital lease.

The standard references OMB Circular No. A-11, *Preparation and Submission of Annual Budget Estimates*, and Circular A-94, *Guidelines and Discount Rates for Benefit-Cost Analysis of Federal Programs*. Circular A-11 explains the measurement of budget authority, outlays, and debt for lease-purchases and capital leases. Circular A-94 presents the requirements under which a lease-purchase or capital lease must be justified.

SFFAS No. 6 discusses the accounting for PP&E, which includes assets acquired through capital leases.

How is FASAB guidance different from others?

In contrast to the limited guidance on leases provided by FASAB, a plethora of guidance on the subject has been written by other standard-setting bodies. It has been said that, "Leases have been the subject of more accounting standards than any other single topic."[6] This is a reflection of the popularity of using leases to acquire assets, the increasing complexity and obfuscation of leasing agreements, and the quest to standardize the accounting for lease transactions.

FASB's basic lease accounting requirements are in SFAS No. 13, *Accounting for Leases*, issued in 1976. Since then, they have issued at least six more statements, six interpretations, and 11 technical bulletins on leases. GASB's authoritative guidance on leases is captured in the National Council on Governmental Accounting Statement (NCGAS) 5, *Accounting and Financial Reporting Principles for Lease Agreements of State and Local Governments*, issued in December 1982. Except for specific guidance to account and report on: Operating leases with scheduled rent increases, [7] fiscal funding or cancellation clauses, [8] and leases between state and local governments and public authorities [9] GASB essentially adopts FASB's SFAS 13, as amended and interpreted, as applicable to state and local governments with consideration given to the distinction between governmental and proprietary funds. The International Federation of Accountants – Public Sector Committee issued its lease standards in International Public Sector Accounting Standards (IPSAS) 13, *Leases*, in December 2001.

Classifications of Leases

Accounting for leases can be divided into two elements -- accounting by the lessor and accounting by the lessee. Lessors report the transfer of rights to use property that they own, and lessees account for and disclose payments for rights to use property that they do not own. [10] Exhibit 1, below, shows the different types of leases recognized by the various standard-setting boards --FASAB, FASB, GASB, and IFAC. OMB guidance is also included for reference.

> In a lease, the right to use tangible property is transferred from the owner, who is the **lessor**, to the **lessee**. A subsequent transfer of the right to use the property during the lease term to another party is a **sublease**.

All the standard-setting boards classify leases for the *lessee* as either a capital lease (IPAC uses the term, finance lease) or an operating lease. Capital leases are considered equivalent to a purchase, while operating leases cover the use of an asset for a period of time and are treated by the lessee as periodic expenses. OMB makes a further distinction and identifies a lease in which ownership is transferred to the Government at or shortly after the end of the lease term as a **lease-purchase**. For other standard-setters such a lease would be considered a capital lease.

A significant difference between FASAB and FASB lease guidance is the classification and treatment of leases by the *lessor*. FASAB does not provide specific accounting guidance when the Federal government is the lessor. This is because historically the Government has been the lessee in the preponderance of Government lease agreements.

---

[6] Harry I. Wolk, Michael G. Tearney, James L. Dodd, Accounting Theory – A Conceptual and Institutional Approach, page 641.

[7] GASBS 13, ¶1 and ¶4.

[8] NCGAS 5, ¶20.

[9] NCGAS 5, ¶23-26, as amended by GASBS 14.

[10] A. N. Mosick, Intermediate Accounting, 1989, page 992.

For the lessor, FASB, classifies a lease as a sales-type lease, direct financing lease, leveraged lease (a type of direct financing lease), or an operating lease. A sales-type lease is a lease that results in a profit or loss to the lessor at the inception of the lease (the fair value of the leased property is greater or less than its cost or carrying amount). Usually sales-type leases arise when manufacturers or dealers are using a lease as a tool to market their product. When a leased asset's fair value is equal to the cost or carrying amount at the inception of the lease, the lease is considered to be a direct financing lease.

EXHIBIT 1. TYPES OF LEASES RECOGNIZED IN STANDARDS

Type of Lease	FASAB	FASB	GASB [11]	IFAC	OMB
Lessee:					
Capital Lease	Yes	Yes	Yes	Finance Lease	Yes
Lease-Purchase	No	No	No	No	Yes
Operating Lease	Yes	Yes	Yes	Yes	Yes
Lessor:					
Capital Lease	No	See below	See below [12]	Finance Lease	---
Sales-Type Lease	No	Yes	Yes	No	---
Direct-Financing Lease	No	Yes	Yes	No	---
Leveraged Leases	No	Yes	Yes	No	---
Operating Leases	No	Yes	Yes	Yes	---

Capital Lease

FASAB and FASB define a capital lease as a lease that transfers substantially all the benefits and risks of ownership to the lessee [13]. IFAC defines a capital lease similarly,[14] but calls it a "finance lease" rather than a capital lease. OMB defines a capital lease as a lease other than a lease-purchase or an operating lease.

Specific criteria are used to determine whether a lease should be classified as a capital or operating lease. Appendix No. 4, "Comparison of Criteria for Classifying a Lease as a Capital Lease," shows how each standard-setting entity does or does not use each criterion.

The four basic criteria are:

---

[11] Footnote 6 of NCGA (National Council on Governmental Accounting) Statement 1 provides that FASB SFAS No. 13, Accounting for Leases, as amended and interpreted, applies to state and local governments. NCGAS 5 provides additional guidance in defining the accounting and financial reporting requirements for lease agreements of state and local governments.

[12] Although GASB does mention the *lessor* in a *capital lease* agreement (for example in NCGAS5, Par. 10), GASB follows SFFAS13 in which the lessor's lease is classified as a sales-type, direct financing, leveraged lease, or operating lease (per conversation with Ken Shermann, GASB staff).

[13] SFFAS 5, ¶43 and SFFAS 6, ¶20

[14] IPSAS 13, Leases – International Public Sector Accounting Standard, December 2001, ¶7.(b) defines a finance lease as, "a lease that transfers substantially all the risks and rewards incident to ownership of an asset. Title may or may not eventually be transferred."

- **Ownership**. The lease transfers ownership of the property to the lessee by the end of the lease term.
- **Bargain Price Option**. The lease contains an option to purchase the leased property at a bargain price. [15]
- **Estimated Economic Life**. The lease term is equal to or greater than 75 percent of the estimated economic life [16] of the leased property.
- **Fair Value**. The present value of rental and other minimum lease payments, excluding that portion of the payments representing executory costs, equals or exceeds 90 percent of the fair value[17] of the leased property.

The last two criteria do not apply when the beginning of the lease term falls within the last 25 percent of the total estimated economic life of the leased property.

FASAB, FASB, and GASB follow the approach that if, at its inception, one or more of the aforementioned four criteria is met, the lease is a capital lease from the perspective of the lessee. OMB takes a slightly different approach, but reaches generally the same conclusion. OMB identifies six criteria, all of which must be met to be identified as an operating lease for budget scoring purposes.[18]

IFAC takes a broader approach and states that the criteria are examples of situations that would normally lead to a lease being classified as a finance (capital) lease, however, a lease does not need to meet these criteria. The two criteria on ownership and bargain price option are the same as those criteria followed by the other standard-setters. For the criterion on estimated economic life, IFAC states that the lease term is for the *major part of the economic life* of the asset even if

---

[15] SFAS 13, ¶ Bargain purchase option is a provision allowing the lessee, at his option, to purchase the leased property for a price that is sufficiently lower than the expected fair value of the property at the date the option becomes exercisable that exercise of the option appears, at the inception of the lease, to be reasonably assured.

[16] SFFAS No. 6, footnote 23, "Estimated economic life of a leased property" is the estimated remaining period during which the property is expected to be economically usable by one or more users, with normal repairs and maintenance, for the purpose for which it was intended at the inception of the lease, without limitation by the lease term.

[17] SFFAS No. 6, footnote 24, states "Fair value" is the price for which an asset could be bought or sold in an arm's-length transaction between unrelated parties (e.g., between a willing buyer and a willing seller).

[18] Office of Management and Budget, OMB Circular A-11, Appendix B identifies six criteria that a lease must meet to be considered an operating lease (the first four are comparable to the four criteria used by FASAB, FASB, and GASB):

- Ownership remains with lessor during lease term and is not transferred to the Government at, or shortly after, the end of the lease term.
- Lease does not contain a bargain-price purchase option.
- The lease term does not exceed 75 percent of the estimated economic life of the asset.
- The present value of the minimum lease payments over the life of the lease does not exceed 90 percent of the fair market value of the asset at the beginning of the lease term.
- Asset is a general purpose asset rather than being for a special purpose of the Government and is not built to the unique specifications of the Government lessee.
- There is a private sector market for the asset.

An operating lease must meet all six criteria. OMB also provides four additional criteria relating to the level of private sector risk involved in a lease-purchase agreement. For budget purposes, there is a distinction, not made in financial reports, between lease-purchases with more or less risk.

title is not transferred, in lieu of the lease term being equal to or greater than 75% of the estimated economic life. And, rather than the present value of the minimum lease payment equaling or exceeding 90% of the fair value of the leased property, IFAC states that the present value of the minimum lease payments should *amount to at least substantially all of the fair value* of the leased asset. In addition to the four criteria, IFAC provides other criteria or indicators of whether or not a lease is a finance lease:

- Leased assets are of a specialized nature such that only the lessee can use them without major modifications.
- Leased assets cannot easily be replaced by another asset.
- If lessee can cancel the lease, lessor's losses associated with cancellation are borne by the lessee.
- Gains or losses from the fluctuation in the fair value of the residual fall to the lessee.
- Lessee can continue the lease for a secondary period at a rent that is substantially lower than market rent.

In summary, the criteria used to determine whether a lease is a capital or operating lease is essentially the same for FASAB, FASB, and GASB. IFAC is less proscriptive and provides additional criteria to use in determining a capital lease. While IFAC uses the term "finance" rather than a capital lease, all four of the standard-setting bodies define a capital lease as one in which the risks and benefits of ownership are transferred to the lessee and should be accounted for as the acquisition of an asset and the incurrence of an obligation by the lessee.

Sales-Type Lease, Direct Financing Lease, and Leveraged Lease

When a lease transfers substantially all of the benefits and risks of ownership to the lessee, FASB considers the lease to be a sale or financing arrangement to the lessor and classifies the lease as a sales-type lease, direct financing lease, or leveraged lease (a type of direct financing lease). Appendix No. 5, "Determining Lessor's Type of Lease – FASB" shows the evaluation process that can be used by a lessor to classify a lease.

When the fair value of the lease is different from its carrying amount, the lease is a **sales-type lease** when real estate is involved and ownership of the asset is transferred, or when real estate is NOT involved, but the lease meets one of the aforementioned four classification criteria and both of two additional criteria.

Two additional criteria must be met:
(1) Collectibility of minimum lease payments is reasonably predictable, and
(2) No important uncertainties surround the amount of unreimbursable costs yet to be incurred by the lessor under the lease.

If there is not an ownership transfer for real estate, or, if the lease does not meet both additional criteria for non-real estate leases, the lease is classified as an operating lease.

If the fair value of the lease is the SAME as its carrying amount and if the lease meets the two additional criteria, the lease is a **direct financing lease**. If real estate is involved the direct financing could be classified as a

leveraged lease if it meets additional criteria[19]. Basically, a leveraged lease involves a long-term creditor who provides nonrecourse financing to the lessor for a leasing transaction between the lessee and the lessor. When the lease does not meet the two additional criteria, it is classified as an operating lease.

Operating Lease

FASAB defines an operating lease as a lease in which the Federal entity does not assume the risks of ownership of the property, plant, and equipment (PP&E)[20]. It is an agreement conveying the right to use property for a limited time in exchange for periodic rental payments. [21]

How does the *lessee* report and account for leases?

Leases are disclosed in the footnotes of agencies' financial statements as required by OMB Bulletin No. 01-09, *Form and Content of Agency Financial Statements.*[22] As a lessee, agencies must provide a summary of the assets under capital lease by major asset category, a description of lease arrangements, and information on future payments. Appendix No. 6 is an extract from Bulletin No. 01-09, which shows the lease information that is disclosed in a footnote to the financial statements.

Capital Lease

Capital leases are reported in the Statement of Financial Position (balance sheet) as an asset under PP&E, and a liability, e.g., Capital Lease Liability. The leased asset is recognized at its acquisition cost when there is agreement between the lessee and the lessor. The amount recorded by the lessee as an asset and an obligation under a capital lease is the present value of the minimum lease payments during the lease term, excluding executory costs,[23] which are expensed by the lessee. However, if this amount exceeds the fair value of the leased asset at the inception of the lease, the amount recorded should be the fair value of the asset. Appendix No. 7, "Accounting for a Capital Lease by a Lessee," shows the steps taken by a lessee to account for a capital lease.

---

[19] FASB, Accounting for Leases a Codification as of October 1, 1998, page 7. A leveraged lease is a direct financing lease that additionally has all of the following characteristics:
   a. It involves at least three parties: a lessee, a long-term creditor, and a lessor.
   b. The financing provided by the long-term creditor is substantial to the transaction and is nonrecourse to the lessor.
   c. The lessor's net investment declines during the early years and increases during the later years of the lease term.
   d. Any investment tax credit retained by the lessor is accounted for as one of the cash flow components of the lease.
[20] SFFAS No. 6, footnote 22.
[21] FASAB Consolidated Glossary.
[22] OMB Bulletin No. 01-09, Form and Content of Agency Financial Statements, September 25, 2001, §9.17 Note 17 Leases.
[23] SFAS 13. Executory costs are those costs such as insurance, maintenance, and taxes incurred for leased property, whether paid by the lessee or lessor.

The discount rate used to determine the present value of the minimum lease payments would be the lesser of the following two rates:

(1) Lessee's incremental borrowing rate, which is the Treasury borrowing rate for securities of similar maturity to the term of the lease; or
(2) The implicit rate used by the lessor.

FASB, GASB, and IFAC recommend comparable accounting for capital leases, except that FASAB specifically defines the lessee's incremental borrowing rate as Treasury's borrowing rate.

The amortization expense and the related interest expense for a capital lease are included in the Statement of Net Cost.[24] Except for land, which is a nondepreciable asset, the acquisition cost is charged to expense through depreciation over the shorter of the useful life of the asset or the lease term.[25] As lease payments are made, the interest expense is recognized.[26] Appendix No. 8, "Illustrative Capital Lease Scenario"[27] shows the budgetary and proprietary journal entries for a capital lease agreement and their reflection in an agency's financial statements.

FASB provides additional guidance to account for a change in the lease provisions, a renewal or extension of an existing lease, and a termination of a lease prior to its expiration.[28]

Operating Lease

SFFAS 1 addresses rental payments made by the Federal Government to a lessor. Rents due to other entities are accounts payable. Rents paid at the beginning of a rental period are typical prepaid expenses. Advances and prepayments should be recorded as assets and reduced when goods or services are received, contract terms are met, progress is made under a contract, or prepaid expenses expire. Appendix No. 9, "Illustrative Scenario for an Operating Lease with a Cancellation Clause"[29] shows the journal entries to account for an operating lease with a

---

[24] Treasury's U.S. Standard General Ledger (USSGL) Approved Scenarios, April 24, 2003, *Capital and Operating Leases*, March 8, 2001 identifies the accounts affected in the pre-closing trial balance and Statement of Net Cost, and the line items in the Statement of Financing and SF 133.

[25] For capital leases where there is not an ownership transfer to the lessee at the end of the lease term, or not a bargain purchase option, FASB instructs the lessee to depreciate the asset over the lease term, and IFAC recommends depreciating the asset over the shorter of lease term or useful life. *FASAB does not provide guidance on whether the leased asset should be depreciated for the lease term,* **or the shorter of lease term or useful life.**

[26] Under budgetary accounting, the budget is obligated in the amount of the present value of the lease payments. Interest expense, which is amortized over the term of the lease, is recorded as an obligation in the budget for the period. Depreciation expense is not recognized in the budget.

[27] Based on U.S. Standard General Ledger (USSGL) draft scenario. While Appendix No. 8 shows the journal entries and statements for year 1, the entire scenario includes 5 years.

[28] SFAS 13, ¶14.

[29] This is a draft scenario provided by Treasury. Appendix No. 9 shows year 1 of a 5-year scenario.

cancellation clause. An operating lease is reported on the Statement of Net Cost as an expense, with the Balance Sheet showing as a liability any accrued lease payments at the end of the reporting period.

How does the _lessor_ report and account for leases?

FASAB does not address the accounting and reporting of leases by lessors. However, the Approved Scenarios in the U.S. Standard General Ledger does show the lessor's journal entries for an operating lease between two Federal agencies.[30] Also, OMB Bulletin No. 01-09, *Form and Content of Agency Financial Statements*, differentiates between the disclosure of leases by the lessee and by the lessor. As a lessor, a Federal agency must provide a description of lease arrangements and information on future projected receipts. See Appendix No. 6.

FASB discusses in depth the accounting and reporting of leases by the lessor. A **sales-type lease** is similar to the sale of a product in exchange for a long-term note. There is a debit to a Receivable and a credit to Sales for the price of the product, and a debit to Cost of Goods Sold and credit to Inventories for the cost of the product. Sales-type leases can have three additional factors: (1) the interest implicit in the minimum lease payments, which are a receivable to the lessor over a period of time, (2) unguaranteed residual value,[31] and (3) initial direct costs, such as commissions, legal fees, and documenting processing costs incurred by the lessor in negotiating and completing the lease contract. In a **direct-financing lease** there is no element of profit at the inception of the lease, and any initial direct costs are expensed, and an equal portion of the unearned interest revenue is recognized as interest revenue in the same accounting period.

In a **leveraged lease**, the lessor records the investment in a leveraged lease net of the nonrecourse debt. The recorded amount is generally (1) rent receivable (net of portion applicable to principal and interest on the nonrecourse debt), (2) the amount of the investment tax credit to be realized in the transaction, (3) any estimated residual value of the leased asset, and (4) a reduction for any unearned revenue items.

FASB also provides guidance in accounting for a change in the provisions of a sales-type or direct-financing lease, a renewal or extension of an existing lease, and a termination of a lease prior to the expiration of the lease term.

FASB guidance for the lessor to account for **operating leases** include the following:

- On the balance sheet, include the leased property with or near property, plant, and equipment, and deduct the accumulated depreciation from the investment in the leased property.
- Depreciate the leased property consistent with the lessor's normal depreciation policy.
- Rent shall be reported as income over the lease term.

---

[30] Treasury, USSGL Approved Scenarios, Capital and Operating Leases, "Illustrative Journal Entries for Operating Lease Between Two Federal Agencies." April 24, 2003
[31] The *unguaranteed* residual value is the portion of the residual value of the leased asset that is the responsibility of the lessor. The *guaranteed* residual value is paid by the lessee to the lessor.

- Initial direct costs shall be deferred and allocated over the lease term; although initial direct costs may be charged to expense as incurred if there is not a material difference.
- For an operating lease involving real estate that would have been a sales-type lease if ownership had transferred to the lessee at the end of the lease term, recognize a loss at the inception of the lease if the fair value of leased property is less than the cost or carrying amount, if different.

What other lease accounting guidance is provided by other standard-setting entities but not covered by FASAB?

Other lease accounting topics covered by standard-setters include:

- Leases Involving Real Estate
- Leases Between Related Parties
- Sale-Leaseback Transactions
- Accounting and Reporting for Subleases and Similar Transactions
- Accounting for Leases in a Business Combination
- Fiscal Clauses

Leases Involving Real Estate

FASB breaks down leases involving real estate into four categories.

(1) Leases involving land only,
(2) Leases involving land and building(s),
(3) Leases involving equipment as well as real estate, and
(4) Leases involving only part of a building.

Appendix No. 10, "Classifying Leases Involving Real Estate" shows the type of lease for every category of lease involving real estate.

If leased property is land only, the lease is classified as an operating lease by the lessee unless ownership is transferred or there is a bargain purchase option, in which case the lease would be a capital lease. If the leased property involves land and building(s), accounting for the lease by the lessee and the lessor depends on which classification criteria are met, whether the fair value of the lease is different from its carrying amount, and the ratio of the fair values of the land and buildings. When a lease involves equipment and real estate, the estimated minimum lease payments for the equipment is estimated and accounted for separately from the real estate by both the lessee and the lessor.

FASB also covers leases whereby only part of a building is leased. If the cost (or carrying amount) and fair value cannot be objectively determined, the lessor should account for the lease as an operating lease, and the lessee should evaluate the lease by applying the estimated economic life criterion. If that criterion is met using the estimated economic life of the building in which the leased premise is located, the leased property is capitalized and accounted for as a capital lease.

It is noteworthy that FASB specifically addresses leases involving terminal space and other airport facilities owned by a governmental unit or authority. Generally because of special provisions associated with these leases, the economic life of such facilities cannot be determined. Also, the concept of fair value is not applicable, and such leases do not provide for a transfer of ownership or a bargain purchase option. Therefore, they are classified as operating leases. FASB Interpretation No. 23, paragraph 8 states that all of the following conditions must be met in order for such a lease to be automatically classified as an operating lease:

a. The leased property is owned by a governmental unit or authority.
b. The leased property is part of a larger facility, such as an airport, operated by or on behalf of the lessor.
c. The leased property is a permanent structure or part of a permanent structure, such as a building, that normally could not be moved to a new location.
d. The lessor, or in some cases a higher governmental authority, has the explicit right under the lease agreement or existing statues or regulations applicable to the leased property to terminate the lease at any time during the lease term, such as by closing the facility containing the leased property or by taking possession of the facility.
e. The lease neither transfers ownership of the leased property to the lessee nor allows the lessee to purchase or otherwise acquire ownership of the leased property.
f. The leased property or equivalent property in the same service area cannot be purchased nor can such property be leased from a nongovernmental unit or authority.

If a leased property does not meet all of these conditions, the lease should be evaluated using the same criteria as is used for classifying other leases involving part of a building.

Leases Between Related Parties [32]

Leases between related parties should be treated the same as similar leases between unrelated parties unless the terms of the lease are significantly affected by the fact that the lessee and the lessor are related. If so, the accounting for the lease should be modified to recognize the economic substance of the lease rather than the legal form. The nature and extent of leasing transactions with related parties must be disclosed.

Sale-leaseback Transactions [33]

In a sale-leaseback transaction, the owner of an asset sells the asset and immediately leases it back. The seller of the asset is the lessee and the buyer who leases it back to the seller is the lessor. If the lease meets one of the four criteria for classifying a lease as a capital lease, the seller-lessee should account for the lease as a capital lease. If none of the four criteria are met, the lease is an operating lease. Any profit or loss on the sale of the asset is deferred and

---

[32] SFAS 13, ¶ 29-31.
[33] SFAS 13, ¶ 32-34, IPSAS 13, ¶ 62-70.

amortized in proportion to the amortization of the leased asset, if a capital lease, [34] or in proportion to the related gross rental charged to expense over the lease term if an operating lease.[35] SFAS 28, paragraph 3 identifies three exceptions.

(1) When the seller-lessee retains only a *minor portion* of the remaining use of the property, the sale and leaseback transactions are treated as *separate transactions*. If the amount of rent is unreasonable based on market conditions, an appropriate amount should be deferred or accrued by adjusting the profit or loss on the sale, and changing the rentals to a reasonable amount.

> The guideline for **minor** is the 90 percent fair value criterion. So that if the present value of a reasonable amount of rental for the leaseback is 10 percent or less of the fair value of the asset sold, the seller-lessee is deemed to have transferred to the buyer-lessor the right to substantially all of the remaining use of the sold property and to have retained only a minor portion of the remaining use.
>
> **Substantially all** is used in the context that the leaseback meets at least one of the four basic classifi-cation criteria to be considered a capital lease.

(2) When the seller-lessee retains *more than a minor portion, but less than substantially all* of the use of the property through a leaseback, and profits from the sale exceed (1) the present value of the minimum lease payments over the lease term if the leaseback is an operating lease, or (2) the recorded amount of the leased asset, if the lease-back is a capital lease, the *profit is recognized on the date of the sale.*

(3) When the *fair value of the property is less than its undepreciated cost*, the *loss is recognized immediately.*

If the lease meets one of the four basic criteria and both of the two additional criteria, [36] the buyer-lessor accounts for the lease as a purchase and a direct financing lease, or a purchase and an operating lease if the criteria are not met.

Specific guidance for *sale-leaseback transactions involving real estate* is provided in FAS 98, *Accounting for Leases*, paragraphs 7-19. It introduces sale-leaseback accounting, whereby the seller-lessee records the sale, removes all property and related liabilities from its balance sheet, recognizes gain or loss from the sale in accordance FASB Statement No. 13, "Accounting for Leases," as amended. The sale-leaseback method of accounting can only be used if the sale-leaseback transaction includes all of the following:

- There exists a normal leaseback, wherein there is active use of the property by the seller-lessee in exchange for rent payments, [37]

---

[34] IPSAS 13, ¶ 63 provides the same guidance, " any excess of sales proceeds over the carrying amount should not be immediately recognized as revenue . . . it should be deferred and amortized over the lease term."

[35] IPSAS 13, ¶65 guidance differs. In a sale/leaseback transaction that results in an operating lease, if the transaction is *at fair value*, any *gain or loss is recognized immediately.* If the sale price is *below fair value*, any *gain or loss is recognized immediately*, except that, *if the loss is compensated by future lease payments at below market price, it should be deferred and amortized* in proportion to the lease payments over the period for which the asset is expected to be used. If the sale price is *above fair value*, the excess over fair value is *deferred and amortized* over the period for which the asset is expected to be used.

[36] The two additional criteria that relate to the predictability of collecting the minimum lease payments and no important uncertainties associated with the unreimbursable costs to be incurred by the lessor.

- There are payment terms and provisions that adequately demonstrate the buyer-lessor's initial and continuing investment in the property, [38] and
- There are payment terms and provisions that transfer all of the other risks and rewards of ownership as demonstrated by the absence of any other continuing involvement by the seller-lessee. [39] If a sale-leaseback transaction does not qualify for sale-leaseback accounting because of continuing involvement by the seller-lessee, it should be accounted for by the deposit method [40] or as a financing.

Subleases and Similar Transactions [41]

FASB provides accounting guidance in the following leasing transactions:

- The lessee re-leases the leased property to a third-party and the lease agreement between the two original parties remains in effect.
- A new lessee is substituted under the original lease agreement.
- A new lessee is substituted through a new agreement, with the original lease agreement cancelled.

Leases in a Business Combination [42]

The classification of a lease will not change as a result of a business combination unless the provisions of the lease are modified. FASB provides specific guidance to account for leases whether a business combination is accounted for by the pooling-of-interests method or the purchase method.

Fiscal Clauses [43]

Many leases with a governmental entity contain a fiscal funding clause that cancels the lease if the governmental entity does not receive the appropriation or other funding authority needed to meet its lease obligations. FASB provides guidance on the impact of such clauses in determining whether the lease is a capital or operating lease. When there is a fiscal funding clause, an assessment must be made to determine the likelihood of the lease being canceled due to a lack of funding. If such an occurrence is *remote*,[44] the lease agreement should be considered a

---

[37] *Normal leaseback* and *active use of the property* are described in SFAS 98, ¶8.

[38] SFAS 66, ¶8-16.

[39] SFAS 98, ¶11-13.

[40] Under the deposit method, lease payments decrease and collections on the buyer-lessor's note, if any, increase the seller-lessee's deposit account. The property and any related debt continue to be included in the seller-lessee's balance sheet, and the seller-lessee continues to depreciate the property.

[41] SFAS 13, ¶35-39.

[42] FIN 21, ¶12-16.

[43] SFFAS 13, ¶5(f), FTB79-10, Fiscal Funding Clauses in Lease Agreements.

[44] Ibid. Paragraph 4 states, "In discussing the likelihood of the occurrence of a future event or events to confirm a loss contingency, paragraph 3 of FASB Statement No. 5, *Accounting for Contingencies*, defines remote as relating to

noncancelable lease. If the likelihood of cancellation is not remote, the lease is considered cancelable, and therefore an operating lease.

GASB elaborates on this [45] by stating that most lease agreements with such clauses are essentially long-term contracts. The likelihood of a government lessee terminating the lease because funds are not available is remote since this would discourage lessors to enter into leases with the government in the future and would adversely affect the receptiveness of lessors to the government's other obligations.

---

conditions when the "chance of the future event or events occurring is slight." The evaluation of the uncertainty of possible lease cancellation should be consistent with that definition."

[45] NCGAS 5, ¶18-21.

USE OF LEASES BY FEDERAL ENTITIES

In the past two decades huge deficits and spending for higher-priority programs have made it difficult for Congress to appropriate the funds needed by Federal agencies to acquire assets. This was especially true for funding costly, long-lived assets such as buildings, ships and aircraft. In response, agencies turned to leases, rather than the outright purchase of an asset, as a means to meet their needs. Before 1991, the budget authority [46] and outlays for all leases were recognized annually, over the lease term as payments were made. Therefore, in contrast to the purchase of an asset, agencies utilizing leases did not have to obtain funding up front from Congress for the entire cost of an asset, and, in the short-run, the acquisition of these assets appeared much less costly than their outright purchase.

The proliferation of lease agreements that seemed designed to circumvent agencies' need to seek appropriations up front, drew concern from the budget community for several reasons. Without the total cost of assets reflected in the budget, the budget did not portray fully the Government's financial commitments. Not all the information was there for decision-makers to monitor and control the budget and investments in assets. Also, by avoiding the need to capture all the costs of the asset up front in the budget process, lower-priority projects were being funded without the usual scrutiny, leading to the inefficient allocation of scarce resources. Finally, the overall cost to the Government is higher, because in the long run, the use of leases to obtain an asset is usually more costly than its outright purchase. Outright purchases are financed through lower interest rate Treasury borrowing, whereas lease-purchases are financed through more costly, private-sector borrowing.

In 1991, new guidelines were issued by OMB to address these concerns. Under the revised guidelines, capital leases and lease-purchases, which essentially provide the Federal agency with ownership of the asset, were scored [47] up front, putting these leases on a budgetary par with actual purchases. On the other hand, operating leases with a cancellation clause and operating leases of self-insuring funds (e.g., GSA) were scored for only the amount of budget authority needed to cover the annual lease payment, and the costs associated with canceling the lease if there was a cancellation clause. If the operating lease did not contain a cancellation clause, the estimated total payments to cover the full term of the contract was scored.

While the new guidelines effectively ceased agencies' use of leases for a time, more recently agencies have been using a succession of operating leases in lieu of a long-term lease to evade the requirement for up-front scoring. The use of operating leases is appropriate as a means to acquire assets needed for a short period of time. However, in lieu of the outright purchase of an

---

[46] *Budget authority* is the authority provided by law to incur financial obligations that will result in immediate or future outlays of Federal funds.

[47] CBO, <u>A CBO Paper -- The Budgetary Treatment of Leases and Public/Private Ventures</u>, February 2003, Footnote 1 states, "Although the term "scoring" is often reserved for the process of identifying and tracking the budget authority and outlays associated with legislative initiatives (legislative scoring), it is sometimes used more broadly to include the activities of OMB as it records the obligations and outlays associated with the actions of federal agencies as they execute the budget."

asset, or even the long-term lease of an asset, using operating leases is almost always a more costly alternative to ownership for the Government.

Why is this important? Budget is concerned with scoring. Accounting is concerned with correctly reflecting the asset on financial statements. This is important because in changing the terms of lease agreements to circumvent the up-front scoring requirement, so that a capital lease is instead an operating lease, the accounting for, and reporting of the asset in the financial statements, has been changed.

Types of Leases and Lease-Like Arrangements

With an environment of limited resources and increasing demands to improve service, Federal managers face a daunting task and numerous challenges in managing the Government's real property portfolio. In response to a congressional request, GAO was asked to compile an inventory of approaches used by Federal agencies to finance capital projects. [48] Their preliminary work is reported in *Budget Issues: Alternative Approaches to Finance Federal Capital*, (GAO-03-1011), issued August 2003. It is based on queries of GAO analysts and on research of publications issued by the Congressional Research Service, CBO, GSA, and professional research organizations. Clarification on specific examples was obtained from Federal officials to a very limited extent.

> **Fully-funded capital projects** receive budget authority up front, before a commitment is made, for the project's full estimated cost or for a stand-alone stage if the project is divisible into stages and the result of that stage is a usable asset.
> Up-front funding is now required for capital leases and lease-purchases. For capital leases, budget authority must be available for the net present value of the total cost of the lease before it can be signed. Because of this scoring requirement, agencies are apt to opt for an operating lease, rather than a capital lease.

In their transmittal letter to Senator Don Nickles, Chairman, Committee on the Budget, dated August 21, 2003, GAO states that their work was not intended to produce a comprehensive list of all capital financing approaches. Rather, GAO believes they identified the major approaches used by Federal agencies to finance capital projects when they are not fully funded. [49]

Ten approaches were identified as being used by one or more of 13 Federal agencies. Of the ten, six appear to relate to leases or lease-like arrangements. These are described by GAO and serve as a convenient way to categorize the Government's lease arrangements.[50]

---

[48] Capital projects included land, improvement projects, and buildings or equipment used in federal operations.
[49] GAO-03-1011, Budget Issues - Alternative Approaches to Finance Federal Capital, August 2003, page 2, footnote 2. The Adequacy of Appropriations Act, 41 U.S.C. §11, and the Anti-deficiency Act, 31 U.S.C. §1341, require an agency to have adequate budget authority before entering into a contract or other obligation for payment. GAO advocates full funding as the best way to ensure that commitments embodied in budget decisions are recognized and to maintain government-wide fiscal control. The difference between the two is that the acts apply to individual contracts, while full, up-front funding relates to a useful segment or an entire project, which can be several contracts. For example, full funding would require budget authority to build a whole ship, while the acts' would require budget authority for a single contract to build a part of the ship.
[50] Ibid.

Operating Leases

An operating lease gives the federal government the use of an asset for a specified period of time, but the ownership of the asset remains with the lessor. As mentioned previously, using an operating lease to acquire the use of an asset for a specified, limited period of time is generally appropriate. However, concern arises when agencies set lease terms to meet the requirements of an operating lease rather than purchasing the asset outright or entering into a capital lease agreement. Following are examples of operating leases used for long-term needs:

Patent and Trademark Office (PTO) Building

- In 1995, Congressional committees authorized the competitive procurement of a 20-year operating lease for 2.2 million square feet to consolidate PTO. Neither user fees nor taxpayer funding was available to construct or purchase a new PTO facility.
- On June 1, 2000 GSA signed a 20-year lease to build space to suit GSA/PTO needs. Lease was valued at $1.24 billion, ($62 million annually), plus operating expenses and taxes.
- Only annual payments are scored in each year of the lease. If the lease had been considered a capital lease, the net present value of $1.24 billion would have been appropriated and scored in fiscal year 2003.
- Under OMB's scoring criteria, the PTO lease was considered an operating lease.
- While concluding that the operating lease was not a cost-effective alternative, GAO did agree that the value of the total lease payment was less than 90 percent of the building's fair value, meeting a key criterion for an operating lease.[51]

Department of Transportation Headquarters Building

- GSA will sell 11 acres of land for $40 million to a private partnership.
- The private partnership will develop a new DOT complex, including 1.35 million square feet of office space that GSA will lease for 15 years for DOT headquarters.
- Normally GSA enters into 20-year leases. However, due to the high rental rates in Washington, a 20-year lease would probably not satisfy the 90 percent criterion for being an operating lease. GSA reduced the lease term to 15 years.

Boeing 767 Tankers

- Congress included language in DOD's FY 2002 appropriations act allowing the Air Force to lease Boeing 767 aircraft and convert them to replace its KC-135 mid-air refueling tankers.

---

[51] GAO, GAO-01-578R, Acquisition of Leased Space for the U.S. Patent and Trademark Office, June 2001.

- Air Force plans to obtain refueling tankers through a 6-year operating lease.
- At the end of the lease term, the Air Force would have the option to purchase the aircraft for a specified, negotiated price.
- In a July 10, 2003, report to the Senate Committee on Armed Services, the Air Force estimated that it would cost $150 million less to purchase the aircraft than to lease them.
- CBO believes that this is significantly understated and the lease-buy strategy would cost $21.5 billion, while an outright purchase of the aircraft would cost $15.9 billion. [52]

Sale-Leaseback

When a federal agency sells an asset and then leases back some or all of the asset from the purchaser, it is a sale-leaseback agreement. Such an arrangement might occur when the agency does not need to use the entire building or when an agency's property needs renovation. In the latter case, the agency may transfer renovation costs to the purchaser, then lease back the property after improvements have been made. While agencies generally are not permitted to keep the proceeds from the sale of assets unless authorized by legislation, Congress has authorized GSA to credit the Federal Buildings Fund with proceeds from the sale of Federal property. Over the long run, sale-leaseback agreements are usually more expensive, and renovations undertaken by the private sector are more costly than those financed by Treasury borrowing. GAO identified one case of a sale-leaseback arrangement.

Charlestown, WV, Federal Building

- Congress included language in an appropriation bill, approving the sale and leaseback of the Byrd Courthouse, and allowing GSA to retain funds from the sale of the building.
- GSA sold the Federal building to a developer for $3.5 million.
- The developer made a commitment to upgrade the building for $11 million and GSA committed to leasing back a portion of the building for 20 years.

Lease-Leaseback

In a lease-leaseback agreement the government agency purchases an asset, the agency then leases out the same asset to a private entity for a fixed time period in return for a lump sum payment, and finally the agency leases back the use of the same asset. The agency maintains ownership and control of the assets. GAO found three such arrangements; all relating to the leasing of combustion turbines by the Tennessee Valley Authority, (TVA), a wholly-owned government corporation.

- The lease-leaseback arrangements provide TVA with financial flexibility because the contract has early buyout and termination options.

---

[52] Congressional Budget Office, Letter to Senator Don Nickels dated August 26, 2003, Assessment of the Air Force's Plan to Acquire 100 Boeing Tanker Aircraft.

- TVA can relinquish the property to the private entity at the end of the lease, with the private entity bearing the residual value of the asset.
- The private entity is entitled to certain tax benefits, some of which are passed to TVA in the form of more favorable financing rates.

Public-Private Partnerships

While a public-private partnership can relate to many different types of partnership arrangements, generally, a public-private partnership is an arrangement whereby the Federal Government contributes real property and a private entity contributes capital and borrowing ability to redevelop or renovate the real property. In their report, *Budget Issues: Alternative Approaches to Finance Federal Capital*, GAO stated that they identified 54 public-private partnership arrangements. These arrangements are typically used when a Federal agency has excess capacity, or when existing facilities do not satisfy current or future needs. The capital and expertise of the private sector are leveraged to improve or redevelop Federal real property assets. Generally, public-private partnerships "involve a government agency contracting with a private partner to renovate, construct, operate, maintain and/or manage a facility or system, in part or in whole, that provides a public service."[53]

Under these partnerships, ownership of the asset may be retained by the Government, but the private partner generally invests its own capital to design and develop the asset. The private partner may be a non-profit organization, a for-profit business, or in some cases a state and local government. GAO found predominately three categories of partnerships: [54]

o Lease/develop/operate. An agency leases a facility from a private partner that invests its own capital to renovate, modernize, and/or expand the facility. The private partner then operates it under a contract with the Federal agency.

o Lease/purchase. Often used for new construction, a private partner finances and builds a facility that is leased to a Federal agency. At the end of the lease term, the agency owns the facility or purchases it at the remaining unpaid balance. The facility may be operated by either the Federal agency or the private partner during the term of the lease.

o Contract Services. There are two types of contract services: (1) operations and maintenance; and (2) operations, maintenance, and management. Under operations and maintenance, the Federal partner contracts with a private partner to provide and/or maintain a specific service or facility. Under the latter, the Federal partner contracts with a private partner to operate, maintain, and manage a facility or system. Under both scenarios the Federal partner retains ownership.

GAO also mentions another type of partnership--Design/build/operate, wherein, a single contract is awarded for the design, construction, and operation of a capital improvement.

---

[53] GAO/GGD-99-23, Public-Private Partnerships - Key Elements of Federal Building and Facility Partnerships, February 1999. page 1.
[54] Ibid. page 5.

Public private partnerships include outleases and share-in-savings contracts, which are alternative financing approaches discussed later.

Potential benefits to the Federal Government from using public-private partnerships include: [55]

- utilization of the untapped value of real property,
- conversion of buildings that are currently a net cost to GSA into net revenue producers,
- attainment of efficient and repaired Federal space,
- reduction of costs incurred in functionally inefficient buildings,
- protection of public interests in historic properties, and
- creation of financial returns for the Government.

Veterans Affairs - Houston Regional Office Collocation

- VA needed to relocate its regional office.
- VA negotiated a 35-year enhanced-use lease with a local developer to design, build, and maintain the Houston VA regional office building, add 500 parking spaces, and develop and maintain the remainder of VA-owned site with commercial buildings.
- VA agreed, following its construction, to lease-purchase the office building within a 1-year period.
- VA states taxpayers saved over $6 million in construction costs and generated an additional $10 million savings in operating costs.
- At the end of the 35-year lease, VA will own the commercial properties.
- VA also received a small portion of developer's profits from the commercial properties.

Veterans Affairs - Office Collocation and Parking Garage, Chicago

- VA needed additional office and parking space.
- A trust was established with VA as the sole beneficiary.
- VA provided the trust with a 35-year lease for a site next to the VA Medical Center.
- On behalf of the trust, a developer will build and manage the office building and parking garage.
- To pay for the design and construction of the facilities, the trust borrows through a development authority that issues $59 million in taxable revenue bonds.
- VA signed short-term operating leases to use space.
- VA payments cover amortization and interest on the trust's debt and expenses.
- VA can purchase the building from the trust at any time.
- Average annual cost to VA for the new office space and parking is projected to be 50 percent less than rates for comparable facilities.

---

[55] GAO-02-45T, Public-Private Partnerships - Factors to Consider When Deliberating Governmental Use as a Real Property Management Tool, October 1, 2001, page 4.

Oak Ridge National Laboratory

- Department of Energy (DOE) needed to replace deteriorating buildings at the Oak Ridge National Laboratory, but did not have the funds to do so.
- DOE designated Federal land next to the Laboratory as excess and conveyed it to a developer, who would finance and oversee the construction of new buildings, then lease the new buildings to DOE's prime contractor.
- A quitclaim deed [56] was used with a 30-year "payback plus profit" term. The private developer offers no-cost repurchase or reacquisition rights to the Federal government for the land and facilities.
- Government reimburses lease payments to DOE's prime contractor.

Outleases

GAO identified 36 outlease arrangements. In these arrangements, the Government is the lessor and excess or underused properties are outleased to the private sector, shifting the cost of maintenance and restoration to the private sector lessee. The National Historic Preservation Act authorizes agencies to use lease proceeds of historic properties to offset the costs of maintaining and repairing other historic properties. Consequently, historic, run-down, Federal properties are good candidates for outleasing.

Galveston Customhouse

- Galveston Customhouse is one of the oldest Federal buildings west of the Mississippi River with its interior in bad condition. Because of its historical significance it was not to be disposed.
- GSA leased out the building to the Galveston Historical Foundation for 60 years. In turn, the Foundation will preserve and restore the customhouse. The restored customhouse will house the Foundation's headquarters and a visitor center.
- GSA no longer has to pay the $162,000 per year cost of operating the property, and did not have to pay the $1 million restoration and repair costs.

Maine Lights Program

- The Coast Guard owns many lighthouses that it is unable to maintain.
- Under the Maine Lights Program 28 historic lighthouses were leased to various organizations that will ensure their maintenance, repair, and care.
- Lease proceeds may be used to offset expenses associated with other historic properties owned by the Coast Guard.
- Coast Guard avoids $3 to $5 million in annual repair and maintenance costs.

---

[56] A quitclaim deed is a legal instrument used to release one party's right, title, or interest to another without providing a guarantee or warranty of title.

<u>U.S. Tariff Building</u>

- After having been vacant for several years, GSA leased the U.S. Tariff Building to a private sector group for 60 years.
- The private sector group restored the building, converting it into a hotel with restaurants, retail space, and meeting rooms. The group paid $32 million to renovate the interior of the building, using the 20 percent Federal historic rehabilitation tax credit to finance a portion of the costs.
- Rent proceeds support the preservation of other historic GSA properties, and GSA no longer incurs the cost to maintain the property.

Share-in-Savings Contracts

Some Federal agencies work with contractors who purchase and install new energy systems in Federal buildings. Agencies then pay back the contractors over time for the equipment plus a percentage of the energy costs saved as a result of the more efficient energy systems and relief of in-house maintenance costs.

<u>Eisenhower Center</u>

- A contractor installed $300,000 of new equipment that will allow more efficient energy management, and special lighting to protect archive records.
- The contractor will be reimbursed for the equipment and financing costs and receive 50 percent of the energy savings.

<u>Heating, Ventilation and Air Conditioning System Upgrade - Commerce</u>

- Commerce negotiated with the Potomac Electric Power Company to improve the heating, ventilation, and air conditioning system, install energy motors, and retrofit chilled water pumps.
- Costs will be repaid from future energy savings.

Special-Purpose Public/Private Ventures

In their paper,[57] CBO discusses the growing use of special-purpose public/private ventures. In their paper,

> a special-purpose public/private ventures refers to a business entity (such as a corporation, partnership, limited liability company, grantor trust, or other trust) that is created by public and private parties for a single specified purpose and

---

[57] CBO, <u>A CBO Paper: The Budgetary Treatment of Leases and Public/Private Ventures</u>, February 2003

whose activities are predetermined by the contracts and other arrangements between the parties involved. A public/private venture differs from an arm's-length lease or purchase contract in that the government plays a significant role in creating and controlling the venture and the government's claims are subordinate to those of the venture's other creditors. [58]

The Government's control could be through voting rights or positions on government boards or through contractual agreements restricting the activities of the public/private venture to serve the Government. A concern expressed by CBO is that the activities of the special-purpose ventures are being recorded as if the ventures were private entities even though they are typically created, and essentially controlled, by the Federal entity's interests. Thus, for example, none of the costs associated with the borrowing undertaken by the venture, and none of the costs between the venture and the private sector, are captured by the Federal entity.

Public/private ventures are often exceedingly complex financing arrangements in which the existence of a lease or lease payments may not be explicit. In lieu of a lease payment, the arrangement may call for the Government to commit to purchase services, or agree to lease, sell or convey the assets to the venture. Appendix No.11 depicts the participants and flows for one venture and illustrates the complexity of these arrangements. While there is not a "typical" public/private venture, CBO provides examples of some ventures.

DOD's Military Housing

- Starting in 1996, DOD was granted authorities to enter into different types of financial arrangements with private-sector partners to provide housing for military families. These arrangements include direct loans, loan guarantees, outleases of land, rental guarantees, bartering arrangements, direct investments by the Government, and property transfers.
- Typically, the private partner secures private, third-party financing to build or renovate family housing units.
- DOD often provides the venture with a lease for Federal land and control over the housing units.
- Rental payments, paid by the service members and equaling their housing allowance, cover the principal and interest on funds borrowed by the venture to construct or renovate units and the costs to maintain and manage the units.
- As of September 2002, CBO estimates that $2.3 billion in housing will have been obtained through public/private ventures, with only $255 million in obligations being recorded. By 2006, DOD plans to have 123,435 housing units privatized, as compared to 26,166 units throughout the United States in 2002.
- Privatization of housing, rather than using military construction, enables DOD to more quickly acquire the number and quality of on-base housing they need.

---

[58] Ibid. page x.

Other Public/Private Ventures

Two examples of VA's use of their enhanced-use authority are described under the section Public/Private Partnerships. VA has established an Office of Enterprise Development within its Facilities Management Office to promote the use of partnerships and to provide guidance on establishing these arrangements.

CBO also discusses TVA's lease-leaseback approach and the Oak Ridge National Laboratory (both referenced above) as examples of public/private ventures.

Statutory Authority

Federal agencies must have statutory authority to enter into joint partnerships with the private sector. Several agencies, have enabling legislation for specific projects, for example, the National Park Service for the Thoreau Center at the Presidio and for the Fort Mason Foundation.

> As one of the largest owners of property in the world, the U.S. Government owns over 400 buildings and more than half a billion acres of land. Almost all government-owned real estate falls under the jurisdiction of eight Federal entities:
>
> | | |
> |---|---|
> | o Agriculture | o DOD |
> | o Energy | o Interior |
> | o VA | o GSA |
> | o TVA | o Postal Service |
>
> Most are national parks, forests, public lands, and military facilities.

Other agencies have broader statutory authority. In 1991, as part of an "asset management" program, Congress authorized the VA to enter into long-term agreements called "enhanced-use" leases.[59] VA was allowed to enter into leases, up to 75 years, for non-VA uses or activities on VA property as long as the uses or activities were not inconsistent with VA's mission. In return, the VA can receive any combination of cash, services, facilities, or other benefits and use it without further appropriation. The Postal Service has even broader authority "to manage its properties using businesslike arrangements" under the Postal Reorganization Act of 1970.

DOD's leasing authority [60] allows lease proceeds to fund facility maintenance and repair or environmental restoration at the military installation where the property is located and elsewhere. Lease terms must promote national defense or be in the public interest, and the lease may not exceed 5 years without approval of the Service Secretary.

Legislation has been proposed to provide GSA with the authority to pursue funding alternatives, when beneficial to the Federal Government. As the Government's landlord, GSA plays a central role in providing office space to other agencies, and managing the government's real property and fleet of vehicles. The agency owns about 1,200 buildings and leases space at about 8,000 different locations that is subleased to other Federal agencies. The "occupancy agreements"

---

[59] P.L. 102-86 (38 U.S.C. § 8161-8169).
[60] 38 U.S.C. § 8161-8169 and 10 U.S.C. § 2667.

covering the sublease arrangements generally allow federal agencies to terminate the lease at any time within 120 days.

Two proposed bills would enhance the authority of GSA and other "land-holding agencies" [61] to enter into lease and lease-like arrangements.

Public Private Partnership Act of 2003

H.R. 2573, "Public Private Partnership Act of 2003" would allow GSA to convey interests in real property, by lease or exchange, to a non-Federal entity.

- GSA may enter into agreements with non-Federal entities to provide for the acquisition, lease, construction, rehabilitation, operation, maintenance, or use of Federal real property.
- For real property held by another landholding agency, GSA may enter into an agreement with a non-Federal entity at the landholding agency's written request.
- Before entering into an agreement, GSA must submit a report to Congress on the proposed agreement.
- The primary purpose of the agreement is to enhance the value of the Government's real property.
- The term of the agreement can be no longer than 50 years.
- Consideration from the non-Federal entity can be in-kind, including providing space, goods, or services to benefit the United States. Services can include construction, repair, remodeling, or other physical improvements to the property, and maintenance of the property, or the provision of office, storage, or other usable space.
- Net proceeds from GSA's real property would be deposited into the Federal Buildings Fund. Proceeds from the real property of other landholding agencies would be deposited into a separate account of the Federal Buildings Fund for the landholding agency.
- GSA's authority to enter into agreements would expire in 6 years.

Federal Property Asset Management Report Act of 2003

The "Federal Property Asset Management Report Act of 2003," H.R. 2548, provides additional authorities to GSA and the head of any landholding agency to manage real property assets.

Interagency Transfers or Exchanges. Real property may be transferred or exchanged between Federal agencies.
Sales to or Exchanges with Non-Federal Sources. Real property may be acquired by selling or exchanging a real property asset or interests with a non-Federal source. However, the agency must first make the property available for transfer or exchange to another Federal agency.

---

[61] "Landholding agency" is defined in H.R. 2548, "Federal Property Asset Management Reform Act of 2003," §2 as any Federal agency that, by specific or general statutory authority, has jurisdiction, custody, and control over property that is real property. Specific exclusions, such as lands held in trust for individual Indians or Indian tribes and National Park System lands, are provided.

<u>Subleases</u>. The unexpired portion of any government lease for real property may be made available to another Federal agency or to any non-Federal entity by lease, permit, or similar arrangement.

<u>Outleases and Public Private Partnerships</u>. Any unused or underused portion of or interest in any real and related personal property may be made available by outlease agreements with other Federal agencies and non-Federal entities.

- An agreement may be made with a partnership, cooperative venture, limited liability company, corporation, trust, sole proprietorship, or other business arrangement.
- Term may not be any longer than 50 years.
- The agency shall receive fair market value.
- An option to leaseback the property to the Federal Government is allowed.
- All leaseback agreements must meet the requirements of an operating lease as specified in relevant OMB circulars.
- Proceeds from partnerships can be retained by the Federal agencies for their capital asset expenditures. Consideration may include any combination of cash or cash equivalents, other property (real or personal), in-kind assets, services related to the transaction, and/or future consideration.
- If the property is no longer needed, the head of the landholding agency may initiate action to transfer all right, title, and interest of the United States in the property to the non-Federal entity, during the term of an outlease involving the development or substantial rehabilitation or renovation of a Federal asset in a business arrangement.
- Comptroller General will submit biennial reports to Congress.
- Authority to enter into agreements will expire in 10 years.
- Senior real property officers will be appointed.
- Performance measures will be used to monitor the effectiveness of Federal real property management, and the results will be reported to Congress.
- GSA will establish and maintain a database of all real property interests.

RELEVANT ISSUES RELATING TO LEASE ACCOUNTING

Department of Justice's Specific Concerns

At the October 2002 FASAB Board meeting, the Department of Justice's Office of Inspector General sought clarification on GSA occupancy agreements, leasehold improvements, cancellation clauses and fiscal funding clauses. Their questions, their position on the questions, and my comments are provided as Appendix No. 12 "Issues: Department of Justice, Office of Inspector General."

Based on my review of occupancy agreements, GSA's 2002 Annual Report, [62] FASAB and FASB guidance, including FASB's Emerging Issues Task Force EITF 01-08, "Determining Whether an Arrangement is a Lease," and on discussions with officials from Justice, and GSA's accounting and asset management areas, we agree with Justice's position that their GSA occupancy agreements should be accounted for, and reported as, leases, along with footnote disclosure. Since leases are defined as an agreement conveying the right to use PP&E, usually for a stated period of time, the occupancy agreements between GSA and Federal agencies would constitute lease agreements. Where GSA has leased space from another entity and subsequently re-leased the space to a customer agency, the arrangement would be considered a sublease. FASAB does not specifically address subleases. However FASB provides guidance to account for and report on subleases. [63] SFAS 13, paragraph 40 states, the new lessee (Justice) shall classify the lease in accordance with the four classification criteria and account for the lease accordingly. For Justice, as the lessee, the accounting treatment for an occupancy agreement would not differ if the building is GSA-owned or leased by GSA for Justice.

FASAB provides limited guidance on accounting for leasehold improvements. SFFAS No. 6, paragraph 18 states that PP&E includes assets acquired through capital leases, *including leasehold improvements* (emphasis added), and with respect to expense recognition and general PP&E, paragraph 37 states:

> Costs which either extend the useful life of an existing general PP&E, or enlarge or improve its capacity shall be capitalized and depreciated/amortized over the remaining useful life of the associated general PP&E.

By inference, the cost of improvements made to property leased under an occupancy agreement should be capitalized also. If Justice pays for the improvement costs, these costs should be capitalized and depreciated over either the period of occupancy or the life of the improvement, whichever is shorter. GSA would treat these costs as an expense. Generally, nonrecurring capital expenditures, over certain thresholds, that add to the service potential of the asset should be capitalized and allocated to future revenue, and expenditures to maintain the asset in good operating condition are recognized as expenses.

---

[62] GSA, Creating a Successful Future at GSA - 2002 Annual Performance and Accountability Report.
[63] SFAS 13, ¶ 35-40.

According to GSA, almost all occupancy agreements contain a cancellation clause that allows agencies to cancel an agreement with 120 days notice. Accordingly, GSA views most occupancy agreements as cancelable and as operating leases. There are a few agreements that are not cancelable because GSA has built the facility to meet an agency's specific needs. For example, laboratories built to the unique requirements of the Drug Enforcement Agency are covered in 10-year, non-cancelable agreements. Leases that are non-cancelable, may be classified as a capital lease if the lease meets one of the four classification criteria.

With respect to a fiscal funding clause, FASB guidance[64] states that an assessment must be made to determine the likelihood of the lease being cancelled due to a lack of funding. If the likelihood of cancellation is remote the lease agreement should be considered a non-cancelable lease; if not, the lease is considered cancelable, and an operating lease. Generally, the likelihood of a government lessee terminating a lease due to a lack of funding is remote. [65]

 I reviewed the issues and proposed recommendations with Justice staff. Justice agrees with all the proposed recommendations.

Global Issues

Following is a discussion of some of the global issues relating to accounting for leases and lease-like arrangements.

<u>**With the growing use of operating leases to meet long-term commitments, should the accounting, and reporting of such leases be revised?**</u>

Whether a lease is classified as a capital lease or operating lease can have a significant impact on financial reporting. In a capital lease, an asset and liability are recognized on the balance sheet, and in an operating lease, the lease payments are recognized as an expense on the income statement (or Statement of Net Cost). More and more, there is concern that existing standards do not require the recognition of material assets and liabilities arising from operating leases in lessees' balance sheets, and that the standards have prompted the structuring of financial arrangements to meet the criteria for operating leases.

GAO has long advocated that many GSA operating leases used for long-term needs should be scored and treated on the same basis as purchases. [66] "Applying the principle of full recognition of the long-term costs to all instruments is more likely to promote the emergency of the most

---

[64] SFFAS 13, ¶ 5(f), FTB 79-10, <u>Fiscal Funding Clauses in Lease Agreements</u>.

[65] NCGAS 5, ¶ 18-21.

[66] GAO, GAO/T-AIMD-94-189, <u>Budget Issues: Budget Scorekeeping for Acquisition of Federal Buildings</u>, Statement of Paul L. Posner, Director, Budget Issues, Accounting and Information Management Division, September 20, 1994; GAO/GGD-97-148R "Comparison of GSA Cost Estimates," Letter to Representative James A. Traficant, Jr. August 6, 1997.

cost effective alternative." [67] GAO notes that it would be difficult to agree on what constitutes long-term needs that warrant up-front budgeting treatment, and judgments on long-term needs would be based not on the Government's legal commitment, but on projections for the future. Existing leases would require additional budget authority and budgetary caps on spending would need to be adjusted.

Recently, OMB partially addressed this concern in the July 2003 release of OMB Circular No. A-11[68] by revising the budgetary treatment of leasebacks from public/private partnerships. If there is substantial private-sector participation [69] an agency's lease from a public/private partnership will be *presumed to be a capital lease*. If there is not substantial private-sector participation, the lease is considered government for purposes of the budget. In both cases, budget authority is scored up-front. Exception is given if the Government leases land to a private entity and later leases back the improvements; such a lease may be treated as an operating lease if it meets the criteria for an operating lease.

A new approach [70] has been proposed by a "working group" consisting of Board members and senior staff members of the standard-setting bodies of Australia, Canada, New Zealand, the United Kingdom, and the United States of America, and staff of the International Accounting Standards Committee. [71] The proposed approach would eliminate the "arbitrary" determinants of whether a lease is a financial (capital) or operating lease. Instead, all leases of more than one year would be recognized at their present value. Material assets and liabilities arising from operating leases would be recognized at the beginning of the lease term, and reported in lessees' balance sheets. Reporting on operating leases for lessors would change also. They would report financial assets (representing amounts receivable from the lessee) and residual interests as separate assets.

Presently, the fundamental premise in lease accounting is the transfer to the lessee of substantially all the risks and rewards of ownership. If substantially all the risks and rewards of ownership are not transferred to the lessee, the lease is classified as an operating lease and no

---

[67] GAO, GAO/T-AIMD-GGD-94-43, Public Buildings: Budget Scorekeeping Prompts Difficult Decisions, Statement of L. Nye Stevens, Director of Planning and Reporting, General Government Division, October 28, 1993.0

[68] OMB,OMB Circular No. A-11, Preparation, Submission and Execution of the Budget, Appendix B, "Scoring Lease Purchases and Leases of Capital Assets," July 25, 2003

[69] Ibid, page B-7, "Substantial private participation means (1) the non-Federal partner has a majority ownership share of the partnership and its revenues; (2) the non-Federal partner has contributed at least 20 percent of the total value of the assets owned by the partnership, (3) the Government has not provided indirect guarantees of the project, such as a rental guarantee or a requirement to pay higher rent if it reduces its use of space . . . "

[70] The approach/idea is not new. This approach was advocated in a Position Paper "Financial Reporting in the 1990s and Beyond" issued in December 1993 by the Association for Investment Management and Research. It was also discussed in the Basis for Conclusions published with SFAS 13: "Some members of the Board who support this Statement hold the view that, regardless of whether substantially all the benefits and risks of ownership are transferred, a lease, in transferring for its term the right to use property, gives rise to the acquisition of an asset and the incurrence of an obligation by the lessee which should be reflected in his financial statements."

[71] McGregor, Warren, Accounting for Leases: A New Approach (Recognition by Lessees of Assets and Liabilities Arising Under Lease Contracts), Financial Accounting Standards Board, 1996.
Nailor, Hans and Lennard, Andrew, Leases: Implementation of a New Approach, Financial Accounting Standards Board, 2000.

asset or liability is recognized by the lessee. The new approach suggests that regardless of whether a lease transfers the risks and rewards of ownership to a lessee, the lease gives rise to the acquisition of an asset (the right to use an asset for the lease term) and the incurrence of a liability (the obligation to make the payments required by the lease). While the lessee usually cannot pledge or dispose of the asset, "nonetheless, the right granted by the lease to use the property is a source of economic benefits controlled by the lessee and, as such, is an asset."[72] More information on this approach and issues relating to implementation can be found in *Leases: Implementation of a New Approach* by Hans Nailor and Andrew Lennard.[73]

The International Accounting Standards Board (IASB) plans to undertake a leasing project to develop a single method of accounting for leases that would not be dependent on the distinction between an operating and finance (capital) lease. Initially the project will address leases of property, plant, and equipment, and subsequently leases of intangible assets. Based on a conversation with IASB staff, they anticipate recommending the aforementioned new approach. A review of the issues will be compiled towards the end of this year and an exposure draft is anticipated in 2006.

How do you determine whether an arrangement is a lease?

With the growing complexity of arrangements, both in the private and public sector, it is often very difficult to determine whether or not an arrangement involves a lease agreement. Some guidance is provided in the Emerging Issues Task Force (EITF)'s Issue No. 01-08, "Determining Whether an Arrangement Contains a Lease" which was ratified at its May 28, 2003 Board meeting. Originally the issue was raised during the Task Force's deliberations on accounting for energy trading activities, but later the Task Force expanded the scope of the issue beyond energy-related contracts. Some of the key points of the abstract from the September 11-12, 2002 meeting [74] include:

- Evaluation of whether an arrangement conveys the right to use PP&E should be based on the substance of an arrangement.
- Property that is the subject of a lease must be specified (explicitly or implicitly) either at inception of the arrangement or at the beginning of the lease term.
- PP&E, as used in SFAS 13, includes land and/or depreciable assets.
- It was generally agreed that when PP&E is explicitly identified and the benefits of PP&E are conveyed based on the passage of time, the arrangement is likely a lease.
- In lieu of the passage of time, a lease arrangement can provide for a specified measure of use (e.g., number of units produced).
- Difficulty arises when the PP&E is not explicitly identified and/or the benefits of PP&E are conveyed based on the output of the PP&E.
- An agreement conveys the ***right to use*** PP&E if:

---

[72] Ibid., page 4.

[73] Ibid.

[74] Staff was unable to obtain the ratified version, so the version discussed pursuant to the September 2002 meeting and available in the GAO Audit Library was reviewed.

a. **PP&E is specified either explicitly or implicitly**, and
b. The arrangement **conveys the right to control the use** of the PP&E. The right to control the use of the PP&E is conveyed if the purchaser can either:

    (1) Operate the PP&E or direct others to operate the PP&E, or
    (2) Control access to the PP&E. If the seller or another third party can use the PP&E concurrently to provide services to others, the right to control the use of the PP&E is NOT conveyed.

Examples of the right to *operate or direct others to operate* the PP&E include the ability to:

(1) Fire and replace the asset's operator while obtaining the output of the asset
(2) Approve significant operating policies with respect to operating the asset
(3) Specify significant operating policies and procedures in the arrangement with the owner/seller having no ability to change such policies and procedures.

Conditions indicative of the ability to *control access* include:

(1) Purchaser has use of PP&E that is an integral part of the purchaser's facilities
(2) Owner/seller is not able to use the PP&E to provide goods or services to others (or for itself) without the purchaser's consent
(3) The PP&E may not be used concurrently (at the discretion of the owner/seller or another third party) to provide significant services to entities unrelated to the purchaser.

If none of the above indicators of the purchaser's right to control the use of the PP&E are present, any of the **following factors result in the presumption that the purchaser has the right** to use the PP&E:

a. Purchaser has a contract to take substantially all of the output of the PP&E for a period of time or stated output, or the purchaser has the right of first refusal or the right to restrict the sale of output.
b. Purchaser guarantees the future value of the PP&E.
c. Purchaser has a bargain purchase option to acquire the PP&E.

The arrangement is not a lease if both of the following criteria are met:

a. Based on the pricing, the owner/seller does not recover substantially all of its costs to own or operate the PP&E.
b. The owner/seller has the ability to pay its financial obligations under the contract and is required to pay substantive damages if the purchaser fails to deliver.

In a public/private venture, should the special-purpose entity that is essentially established and controlled by the Federal agency, be consolidated into an agency's financial statements?

In many public/private ventures, a special entity, essentially under the control of the public partner, is established to obtain financing for, and/or design, construct, and operate, a Federal asset. Yet, there is no recognition or disclosure of the special entity in the agency's financial statements. An argument could be made that as the primary beneficiary of the special entity, its assets, liabilities, and results of activities should be consolidated in the financial statements of the Federal agency. This would provide readers of financial statements with a more complete picture of the agency's resources, obligations, risks, and opportunities.

EITF Issue No. 90-15 discussed the situation where a lessee enters into a lease designed to qualify as an operating lease, but certain characteristics of the arrangement, as provided below, call into question whether the operating lease treatment is appropriate.

1. Lessee guarantees residual value and participates in both risks and rewards associated with ownership of the leased property.
2. Purchase options exist.
3. Special-purpose entity (SPE) lessor lacks economic substance.
4. Property is constructed to lessee's specifications.
5. Lease payments adjusted for final construction costs.

The Task Force concluded that a lessee is required to consolidate a SPE lessor and report the assets, liabilities, results of operations, and cash flows of the SPE in the leesee's financial statement, when all of the following conditions exist:

1. Substantially all of the activities of the SPE involve assets that are to be leased to a single lessee.
2. The expected substantive residual risks and substantially all the residual rewards of the leased asset(s) and the obligation imposed by the underlying debt of the SPE reside directly or indirectly with the lessee through such means as:

    - the lease agreement
    - a residual value guarantee
    - a guarantee of the SPE's debt
    - an option granting the lessee a right to (1) purchase the leased asset at a fixed price or at a defined price other than fair value determined at the date of exercise or (2) receive any of the lessor's sales proceeds in excess of a stipulated amount.

3. The owner(s) of record of the SPE has not made an initial substantive residual equity capital investment that is at risk during the entire term of the lease.

More recently, FASB Interpretation No. 46, *Consolidation of Variable Interest Entities* was issued this past January, interpreting ARB No. 51, which requires an entity's consolidated financial statements to include subsidiaries in which the enterprise has a controlling financial interest. In the past the determination of whether an enterprise had a controlling financial interest was based on a majority voting interest. But this has not been an effective criterion for determining controlling financial interest. FIN No. 46 explains how to identify variable interest entities and provides clarification on how an entity can assess its interests in a variable interest entity to determine whether to consolidate the entity. An entity that consolidates a variable interest entity would be the primary beneficiary of the variable interest entity. The primary beneficiary is the entity that absorbs a majority of the variable interest entity's expected losses, receives a majority of the expected residual returns, or both.

While further analysis is needed, preliminary discussions with FASB and CBO staff indicate that the special-purpose entities in public/private ventures are often comparable to the variable interest entities that are candidates for consolidation. One of the difficulties in implementation has been that the primary beneficiary does not have access to the information that is required for disclosure. In the future, contract terms are to be written to include access to the needed information.

Should Federal agencies disclose information on operating leases with cancellation clauses? Do they?

SFAS 13 requires supplemental disclosures for operating leases without cancellation clauses, but not for operating leases with cancellation clauses. It is unclear why this is so, except perhaps since SFAS 13 required many more leases to be considered capital leases and disclosed, it was felt that the need for supplement information on leases with cancellation clauses was not as great.[75] Federal agencies disclose information on operating leases as provided in OMB Bulletin No. 01-09, Form and Content of Agency Financial Statements.[76] However, it is uncertain to what extent agencies are reporting or not reporting operating leases with cancellation clauses. For the Federal Government, there are many leases/subleases that have cancellation clauses, GSA occupancy agreements come to mind. If agencies are not disclosing information on leases with cancellation clauses, would it be helpful and cost-effective to have agencies report this information?

Does FASAB need to provide additional guidance on leases?

Based on my review of lease standards, agencies inquiries, and the use of leases by Federal agencies, it is clear that FASAB does need to provide additional guidance on certain lease-related topics.

Fiscal Clauses. Many Federal contracts, particularly contracts signed near the end of a fiscal year, contain a fiscal funding clause that cancels the contract if the Federal entity does not receive the appropriation or other funding authority needed to meet its contractual obligations. The impact of a fiscal clause on a lease was one of the issues on which Justice sought guidance. SFAS 13, ¶5(f), as amended, and FTB 79-10, *Fiscal Funding Clauses in Lease Agreements*, provide guidance that can be used as a basis for preparing FASAB guidance.

Leasehold Improvements. FASAB provides guidance on accounting for improvements to PP&E, but does not specifically address leasehold improvements. To ensure that the accounting for leasehold improvements is consistent throughout Government, FASAB should provide guidance

---

[75] Wolk, Harry I.; Tearney, Michael G.; Dodd, James L., Accounting Theory: A Conceptual and Institutional Approach, South-Western College Publishing, fifth edition, Chapter 17. Leases. page 657.
[76] OMB, OMB Bulletin No. 01-09, Form and Content of Agency Financial Statements, September 25, 2001. See Appendix No. 6.

or clarification on capitalizing leasehold improvements over the shorter of the lease term or the life of the leased asset.

Subleases and Similar Transactions. Since almost all of GSA's occupancy agreements with other agencies of their leased properties are in substance, subleases, it would be helpful to provide some guidance on accounting for subleases. Also, in proposed legislation, the ability to sublease the unexpired portion of any government lease for real property to another Federal agency or to any non-Federal entity is being provided as additional authority to landholding agencies. SFAS 13, ¶35-39 can serve as a basis for FASAB guidance. Guidance should be provided when the Government is either the sub-lessor (e.g., GSA) or the sub-lessee (a GSA agency client).

Government as Lessor/Outleasing. It is not unusual for a Federal agency to be a lessor, however FASAB does not provide guidance on lessor accounting. GAO identified 36 outlease arrangements.[77] Many of these are authorized under the National Historic Preservation Act, which allows agencies to use lease proceeds of historic properties to offset operations and maintenance costs. Consequently, there are a number of leases to the private sector involving historic, run-down, Federal properties. Also, legislation now under consideration would allow agencies to lease any unused or underused portion of or interest in any real and related personal property to other Federal agencies and non-Federal entities. IPSAS 13, *Leases*, pages 16-17, is a good discussion of the circumstances in which the public sector may enter into finance leases as a lessor.

While it is clear that additional guidance should be given on accounting for leases when the Government is the lessor. It will not be easy to require the Federal lessor to classify and account for leases as sales-type, financing-type, or leveraged leases. See discussion below.

Sale-Leaseback/Lease-Leaseback. FASAB and IFAC provide considerable guidance on sale-leaseback transactions, and it has been the topic of a number of issues addressed by FASB's Emerging Issues Task Force.[78] While GAO identified only identified one sale-leaseback arrangement and one lease-leaseback arrangement in their study,[79] these types of transactions are imbedded in many of the public/private partnerships and public/private ventures. FASAB guidance should provide guidance on the accounting for sale-leaseback and lease-leaseback arrangements, at a minimum, accounting guidance should be provided on how to account for any gain or loss.

On other lease-related topics, further study is needed to determine to what extent additional FASAB guidance is needed.

---

[77] GAO, GAO-03-1011, Budget Issues - Alternative Approaches to Finance Federal Capital, August 2003, page 7.
[78] FASB, EITF issues: No. 84-37, Sale-Leaseback Transaction with Repurchase Option, No. 85-16, Leveraged Leases: Real Estate Leases and Sale-Leaseback Transactions, Delayed Equity Contributions by Lessors, No. 89-16, Consideration of Executory Costs in Sale-Leaseback Transactions, No. 90-14, Unsecured Guarantee by Parent of Subsidiary's Lease Payments in a Sale-Leaseback Transaction, No. 90-20, Impact of an Uncollateralized Irrevocable Letter of Credit on a Real Estate Sale-Leaseback Transaction, No. 93-8, Accounting for the Sale and Leaseback of an Asset that is Leased to Another Party, No. D-24, Sale-Leaseback Transactions with Continuing Involvement.
[79] GAO, GAO-03-1011, Op cit., page 6.

Classification of Leases for Lessors. There are Federal leases where the Government is the lessor and leases would meet the FASB criteria for **sales-type, financing-type, and leveraged leases.** *But further study and discussion is needed to determine whether this type of information would be useful and cost beneficial to capture.*

Leases Involving Real Estate. There is considerable FASB guidance relating to the classification of leases involving real estate. (See Appendix No. 10, "Classifying Leases Involving Real Estate.") The type of lease is predicated on whether the lease covers only land, or land and building, or equipment and real estate, or only part of a building. If the leased property is only land, the lease is classified as an operating lease unless there is a transfer of ownership or a bargain purchase option. If a lease includes land and building, the type of lease is dependent on which of the classification criteria is met, if the fair value of the lease is different from its carrying amount, and the ratio of the fair values of the land and buildings. *To what extent should the Federal Government adopt private sector accounting with respect to classifying leases involving real estate?*

Special-Purpose Public/Private Ventures. Both OMB and FASB have recently issued guidance on the treatment of public-private partnerships or special-purpose public/private ventures. As mentioned previously, OMB Circular No. A-11[80] states that if there is substantial private-sector participation, the lease in a public/private partnership is presumed to be a capital lease. Also, FASB Interpretation No. 46, *Consolidation of Variable Interest Entities* reiterates the requirement that variable interest entities be consolidated in the primary beneficiary's financial statements when certain conditions are met. With the increasing use of public/private partnerships and special-purpose public/private ventures, FASAB needs to reevaluate whether or not, and when, a lease that is a component of such an arrangement should be capitalized rather than accounted for as an operating lease, and whether the special purpose entity needs to be consolidated in the financial statements of the Federal agency and the evaluation criteria to be used.

---

[80] OMB,OMB Circular No. A-11, Preparation, Submission and Execution of the Budget, Appendix B, "Scoring Lease Purchases and Leases of Capital Assets," July 25, 2003

NEXT STEPS

By providing background information on what is covered in leasing standards, the use of leases by Federal agencies, and some of the issues relating to leases, this paper should serve as a springboard for further study, analysis and action. Here are some suggestions on the next steps to be taken:

Prepare Staff Position Paper

The concerns raised by Justice can be resolved by interpreting existing FASAB guidance and documenting them in a staff position paper. The narrative in this Research Paper, along with Appendix No. 12 "Issues: Department of Justice, Office of Inspector General," can be the framework for the staff position paper addressing the accounting for GSA occupancy agreements and leasehold improvements.

Expand FASAB Guidance on Leases

There are a number of lease-related topics that should be included in FASAB guidance, either by drafting a separate standard on leases and/or by referencing existing FASB guidance. Possible topics include: fiscal funding clauses, leasehold improvements, subleases, Government as lessor/outleasing, sales-type, financing-type, and leveraged leases, sale-leaseback and lease-leaseback arrangements.

Monitor Status

Keep up with the status of the following:

- IASB leasing project to develop a single method of accounting for leases.
- GAO's review of alternative approaches to finance capital assets (specifically public/private partnerships and share-in-savings contracts).
- EITF abstracts on leases, including Issue No. 01-08, "Determining Whether an Arrangement Contains a Lease" and issues relating to sale-leaseback arrangements and special-purpose entities.
- Current use of public/private partnerships/ventures by agencies.

Further Analysis

- Continue to evaluate agencies' use of leases in individual special-purpose public/private ventures. Review and determine applicability of EITF abstracts relating to such arrangements. [81]

---

[81] FASB, EITF Issues: No. 87-7, <u>Sale of an Asset Subject to a Lease and Nonrecourse Financing: "Wrap Lease Transactions,"</u> No. 90-15, <u>Impact of Nonsubstantive Lessors, Residual Value Guarantees, and Other Provisions in Leasing Transactions</u>, No. 95-6, <u>Accounting by a Real Estate Investment Trust for an Investment in a Service</u>

- Review issues related to new approach and determine applicability to Federal sector.

Establish a Network of Agency Contacts

Establish a network of agency contacts from Treasury, DOD, and other agencies such as VA, Energy, GSA, NASA, Interior, Agriculture, to obtain feedback on:

- How agencies are accounting for, and disclosing, GSA occupancy agreements.
- How agencies are accounting for, and disclosing, leasehold improvements.
- How agencies are disclosing leases with cancellation clauses.
- How agencies are accounting for, and reporting outleases, public/private partnerships and special-purpose public/private ventures.
- Impact of requiring agencies to follow FASB guidance on classifying leases involving real estate.
- Impact of implementing new approach whereby all leases over a year old would be capitalized.

CONCLUSION

There is no question that additional FASAB guidance on lease accounting is needed based on the results of this research phase. The dilemma is how much guidance, and how soon, given limited Staff resources and other project priorities.

Certain agency issues and concerns, including those raised by the Department of Justice, Office of Inspector General, can be addressed forthwith through a Staff position paper. This would interpret and clarify existing FASAB guidance, particularly with respect to GSA occupancy agreements and leasehold improvements.

There are significant gaps in FASAB standards relating to lease accounting. The existing guidance was to be a placeholder until this complex subject could be studied more thoroughly. To assure there is consistent accounting and reporting on leases, guidance should be developed on the impact of fiscal funding clauses on the classification of a lease, and accounting for subleases, the Government as lessor, and sale-leaseback transactions. For these topics, private-sector guidance can be a model for FASAB guidance.

There are billions of dollars in Federal leases involving real estate, but there is not Federal guidance on accounting for leases involving real estate. *Should the Federal sector be required to provide a more detailed accounting for leases involving real estate?*

In the past, there were few situations in which the Government as lessors were involved with sales-type and leveraged leases. However, as more agencies are being held accountable for

---

Corporation, No. 96-21, Implementation Issues in Accounting for Leasing Transactions involving Special-Purpose Entities, No. 97-1, Implementation Issues in Accounting for Lease Transactions, including those involving Special-Purpose Entities, No. 97-10, The Effect of Lessee Involvement in Asset Construction, D-14, Transactions involving Special-Purpose Entities.

better asset management, and are being given the authorities needed to do so, such lease arrangements are occurring and will occur more frequently. To the extent the Federal Government should account for such transactions, FASAB guidance is needed.

Much more difficult to tackle, and with considerable political ramifications, are the broader issues like:

- Eliminating lease classifications and adopting a new approach to capitalize leases that are longer than one year, and

- Determining whether special purpose entities in public/private ventures (also known as variable interest entities) should be consolidated in the public entity's financial statements and whether the leases in such arrangements should be capitalized rather than accounted for as operating leases.

Addressing these exceedingly complex issues will require much effort and time from FASAB Staff and Board.

APPENDICES

APPENDIX NO. 1: CAPITAL AND OPERATING LEASES AND LEASEHOLD IMPROVEMENTS SKELETON PROJECT PLAN RESEARCH PHASE

First Objective: Develop a summary paper that permits staff and the Board to familiarize themselves with lease accounting under FASAB, FASB, GASB and international public sector accounting standards and global issues related to lease accounting. This extends to the standards promulgated by the principle standard setting body as well as the lower level guidance and practice aids available in the profession.

Output:

1. A list of the authoritative literature available (excluding "other literature as described in the GAAP hierarchy)
2. A summary of level A guidance and highlight any differences between FASAB standards and other standards.
3. A list of relevant issues that are addressed by authoritative literature in other domains (FASB) but not here (this list of issues should be coordinated with the Justice IG staff that requested Board action – see minutes of the October 2002 agenda hearing) This list would inform the work in the next phase

Second Objective: Review literature to determine if new uses of leases by federal entities create different and/or more urgent needs for guidance. See the CBO report on leases, articles about DoD leases of jets and partnerships with housing developers for military housing, GAO reports on leasing and the proposed legislation regarding asset management (I will forward by e-mail). If feasible, a review of federal entity reports to determine how they are accounting for these new activities. An alternative is to contact the entities and request a summary of their accounting practices.

Output:

1. A bibliography of resources and articles
2. Examples of the types of lease/partnership activity found at federal entities and how they are accounted for
3. An assessment of whether the activities of federal entities may result in inconsistent accounting absent guidance from FASAB or its staff
4. An assessment of whether the new legislation creates a need for more detailed lease or joint venture or "Special Purpose Entity" guidance.

Recommendation Phase:

We will develop this as the research phase progresses. A task force may be needed to support your recommendation.

APPENDIX NO. 2: LIST OF AUTHORITATIVE LITERATURE

Standard	**Title**
SFFAS 1	*Accounting for Selected Assets and Liabilities*
SFFAS 5	*Accounting for Liabilities of the Federal Government*
SFFAS 6	*Accounting for Property, Plant, and Equipment*
SFAS 13	*Accounting for Leases*
SFAS 22	*Changes in the Provisions of Lease Agreements Resulting from Refundings of Tax-Exempt Debt*
SFAS 23	*Inception of the Lease*
SFAS 27	*Classification of Renewals or Extensions of Existing Sales-Type or Direct Financing Leases*
SFAS 28	*Accounting for Sales with Leasebacks*
SFAS 29	*Determining Contingent Rentals*
SFAS 66	*Account for Sales of Real Estate*
SFAS 71	*Accounting for Effects of Certain Types of Regulation*
SFAS 98	*Accounting for Leases:* • Sale-leaseback Transactions Involving Real Estate • Sales-type leases of real estate • Definition of the Lease Term • Initial Direct Costs of Direct Financing Leases
FIN 19	*Lessee Guarantee of the Residual Value of Leased Property*
FIN 21	*Accounting for Leases in a Business Combination*
FIN 23	*Leases of Certain Property Owned by a Governmental Unit or Authority*
FIN 24	*Leases Involving Only Part of a Building*
FIN 26	*Accounting for Purchase of a Leased Asset by the Lessee During the Term of the Lease*
FIN 27	*Accounting for a Loss on a Sublease*
Fin 46	*Consolidation of Variable Interest Entities*
FTB79-10	*Fiscal Funding Clauses in Lease Agreements*

Standard	Title
FTB79-12	*Interest Rate Used in Calculating the Present Value of Minimum Lease Payments*
FTB79-13	*Applicability of FASB Statement No. 13 to Current Value Financial Statements*
FTB79-14	*Upward Adjustment of Guaranteed Residual Values*
FTB79-15	*Accounting for Loss on a Sublease Not Involving the Disposal of a Segment*
FTB79-16(R)	*Effect of a Change in Income Tax Rate on the Accounting for Leveraged Leases*
FTB79-17	*Reporting Cumulative Effect Adjustment from Retroactive Application of FASB Statement No. 13*
FTB79-18	*Transition Requirement of Certain FASB Amendments and Interpretations of FASB Statement No. 13*
FTB85-3	*Accounting for Operating Leases with Scheduled Rent Increases*
FTB86-2	*Accounting for an Interest in the Residual Value of a Leased Asset:* • Acquired by a Third Party • Retained by a Lessor that Sells the Related Minimum Rental Payments
FTB88-1	*Issues Relating to Accounting for Leases:* • Time Pattern of the Physical Use of the Property in an Operating Lease • Lease Incentives in an Operating Lease • Applicability of Leveraged Lease Accounting to Existing Assets of the Lessor • Money-Over-Money Lease Transactions • Wrap Lease Transactions
NCGAS5	*Accounting and Financial Reporting Principles for Lease Agreements of State and Local Governments*
GASBS13	*Accounting for Operating Leases with Scheduled Rent Increases*
GASBS14	*The Financial Reporting Entity*
IPSAS13	*Leases - International Public Sector Accounting Standard*

APPENDIX NO. 3: LIST OF CONTACTS

Organization	Name	Contact Numbers	Summary of Conversation(s)
CBO	Kathy Gramp	(202) 226-2865	Very helpful. Discussed CBO paper and special purpose public/private ventures.
Treasury	Marilyn Evans Christine Chang	(202) 874-1274 (202) 874-6445	Discussed U.S. Standard General Ledger approved scenario for capital and operating leases, and proposed scenario for Architect of the Capital.
GAO	Carol Henn	(202) 522-5301	Discussed current review of public/private partnerships and past GAO reports on leases/lease-type arrangements.
DOD	Tom Waddell Mike Burke	604-6350, x125 (703) 604-3350	Discussed scope of research project on leasing.
OMB	Gail Zimmerman	(202) 395-3882	Discussed and clarified OMB guidance.
Library of Congress	Marlene Torres	(202) 707-5446	She provided information on NASA leasing via email.
GSA	Ed Gramp Brad Harrison	(202) 501-0593 (202) 708-4625	Discussed accounting for GSA leases and occupancy agreements, cancellation and fiscal funding clauses.
Justice	Marilyn Kessinger Mark Hayes	Mark.L.Hayes@usdoj.gov 616-4523	Discussed DOJ issues & proposed recommendations.
NASA	Al Johnson (Logistics) Lynne Carey (Acctg)	(202) 358-1834 (202) 358-4552	Didn't get to speak to them.
FASB	Sue Bielstein Ann McIntosh	sqbielstein@fasb.org (203) 956-5231	Discussed whether or not there were any on-going projects on leases. Discussed comparability of variable interest entities as addressed in FASB Interpretation No. 45, Consolidation of Variable Interest Entities to Public/Private Ventures.
GASB	Ken Shermann	(203) 847-0700	Verified that GASB essentially follows FASB Statement No. 13.
IASB	Sue Lloyd	slloyd@iasb.org.uk	Discussed IASB leasing project and its status.
Standards and Poor	James Penrose Richard Marino	(212)438-6604 (212) 438-2058	Offered to help understand public/private ventures.

APPENDIX NO. 4: COMPARISON OF CRITERIA FOR CLASSIFYING A LEASE AS A CAPITAL LEASE

Provision	FASAB	FASB	GASB	IFAC	OMB (Circular A-11, Appendix B)
Capital Leases					
Definition	Leases that transfer substantially all the benefits & risks of ownership to the lessee. (SFFAS5, ¶43)	Uses same definition, but capital lease is limited to lessee, not lessor.		A *finance lease* transfers substantially all the risks & rewards incident to ownership of an asset. Title may or may not eventually be transferred.	Any lease other than a lease-purchase or an operating lease. Lease-purchase is a lease in which ownership is transferred to Govt at or shortly after end of lease term.
Capital Lease Criteria	If, at its inception, a lease meets one or more of following criteria, lease is capital lease. (SFFAS5, ¶43)	Same	Follow FASB criteria, though has specific guidance for operating leases with scheduled rent increases.	Although the following are examples of situations that would normally lead to a lease being classified (at lease inception) as a finance lease, a lease does not need to meet all these criteria.	Identifies six criteria that a lease must meet to be considered an operating lease. (Must meet all six criteria)
Capital Lease Criterion- Ownership	Lease transfers ownership of the property to the lessee by the end of the lease term.	Same		Same	Ownership remains with lessor during term of lease & is not trans-ferred to Govt at or shortly after end of lease term.
Capital Lease Criterion-Bargain Price Option	Lease contains an option to purchase the leased property at a bargain price.	Same		Same	Lease does not contain a bargain-price purchase option.
Capital Lease Criterion- Estimated Economic Life	Lease term is equal to or greater than 75% of the estimated economic life of the leased property.	Same		Lease term is for the major part of the economic life of the asset even if title is not transferred.	Lease term does not exceed 75% of the estimated economic life of the asset.

Provision	FASAB	FASB	GASB	IFAC	OMB (Circular A-11, Appendix B)
Capital Lease Criterion-Fair Value	Present value of rental & other minimum lease payments, excluding portion representing executory cost, equals or exceeds 90% of the fair value of the leased property.	Present value at beginning of lease term of minimum lease payments, excluding portion representing executory cost, including any profit thereon, equals or exceeds 90% of excess of the fair value at inception of lease over any related investment tax credit retained by the lessor and expected to be realized.		At lease inception, the present value of the minimum lease payments amounts to at least substantially all of the fair value of the leased asset.	The present value of the minimum lease payments over the life of lease does not exceed 90% of the FMV of asset at the beginning of the lease term.
Capital Lease Criterion-Unique Requirements/ Specialized Nature		Same		Leased assets are of a specialized nature such that only the lessee can use them without major modifications.	Asset is a general purpose asset rather than being for a special purpose of Govt & is not built to unique specifications of the Govt lessee.
Capital Lease Criterion-Private Sector Market					There is a private sector market for the asset.
Criterion-Not Easily Replaced				Leased assets cannot easily be replaced by another asset.	
Criteria Qualifier	Estimated economic life and fair value don't apply when beginning of the lease falls within last 25% of total estimated economic life of the leased property.				
Other Indicator of Capital Lease				If lessee can cancel the lease, lessor's losses associated with cancellation are borne by the lessee.	
Other Indicator of Capital Lease				Gains or losses from the fluctuation in the fair value of the residual fall to lessee.	

Provision	FASAB	FASB	GASB	IFAC	OMB (Circular A-11, Appendix B)
Other Indicator of Capital Lease				Lessee can continue the lease for a secondary period at a rent that is substantially lower than market rent.	

52

APPENDIX NO. 5: DETERMINING LESSOR'S TYPE OF LEASE -FASB

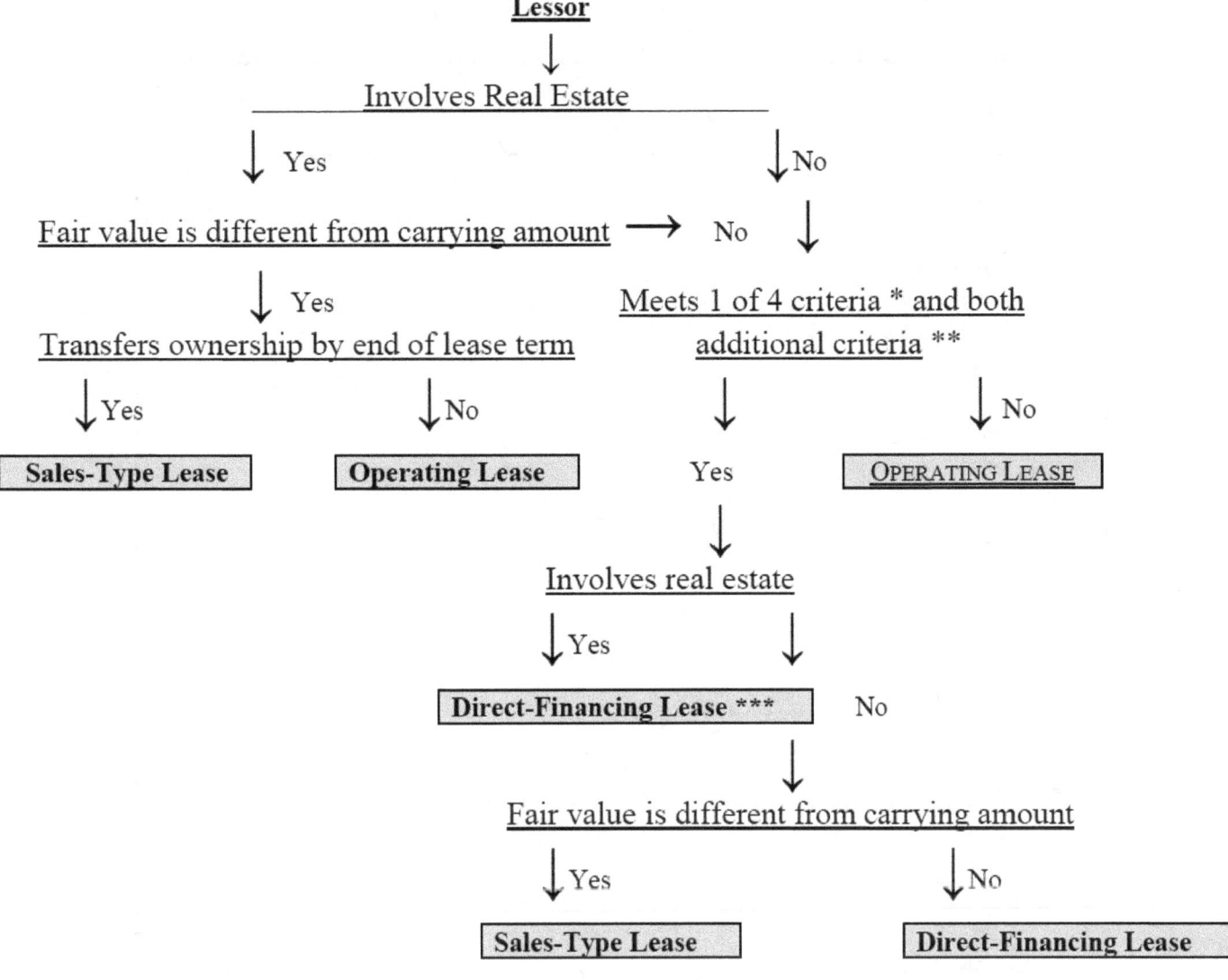

* Must Meet One or More of Following Four Criteria

- Ownership transfers by end of lease term.
- Lease contains an option to purchase leased property at a bargain price.
- Lease term is equal to or greater than 75% of estimated economic life of the leased property.
- Present value of rental & other minimum lease payments, excluding portion representing executory cost, equals or exceeds 90% of the fair value of the leased property.

** Must Meet Both Additional Criteria

- Collectibility of minimum lease payments is reasonably predictable.
- No important uncertainties surround amount of unreimbursable costs yet to be incurred by the lessor under the lease.

*** Unless meets leveraged-lease criteria.

APPENDIX 6: FOOTNOTE DISCLOSURE: EXTRACT FROM OMB BULLETIN NO. 01-09

9.17 Note 17 Leases

Note 17 Leases

A. **Entity as Lessee:**

Capital Leases:				20x2	20x1
Summary of Assets Under Capital Lease:					
Land and Buildings......................................				xxx	xxx
Machinery and Equipment.............................				xxx	xxx
Other..				xxx	xxx
Accumulated Amortization...........................				xxx	xxx

Description of Lease Arrangements: _____

Future Payments Due:

	Asset Category			
Fiscal Year	(1)	(2)	(3)	Totals
Year 1	xxx	xxx	xxx	xxx
Year 2	xxx	xxx	xxx	xxx
Year 3	xxx	xxx	xxx	xxx
Year 4	xxx	xxx	xxx	xxx
Year 5	xxx	xxx	xxx	xxx
After 5 Years	xxx	xxx	xxx	xxx
Total Future Lease Payments	xxx	xxx	xxx	xxx
Less: Imputed Interest	xxx	xxx	xxx	xxx
Less: Executory Costs (e.g., taxes)	xxx	xxx	xxx	xxx
Net Capital Lease Liability	x.xxx	x.xxx	x.xxx	x.xxx

Lease liabilities covered by budgetary resources   x.xxx
Lease liabilities not covered by budgetary resources   x.xxx

Operating Leases:
Description of Lease Arrangements: _____

Future Payments Due:

	Asset Category			
Fiscal Year	(1)	(2)	(3)	Totals
Year 1	xxx	xxx	xxx	xxx
Year 2	xxx	xxx	xxx	xxx
Year 3	xxx	xxx	xxx	xxx
Year 4	xxx	xxx	xxx	xxx
Year 5	xxx	xxx	xxx	xxx
After 5 Years	xxx	xxx	xxx	xxx
Total Future Lease Payments...........	x.xxx	x.xxx	x.xxx	x.xxx

54

B. **Entity as Lessor:**

    Capital Leases:

    Description of Lease Arrangements: _____

    _____

    Future Projected Receipts:

Fiscal Year	Asset Category (1)	(2)	(3)	Totals
Year 1	XXX	XXX	XXX	XXX
Year 2	XXX	XXX	XXX	XXX
Year 3	XXX	XXX	XXX	XXX
Year 4	XXX	XXX	XXX	XXX
Year 5	XXX	XXX	XXX	XXX
After 5 Years	XXX	XXX	XXX	XXX
Total Future Capital Lease Receivables.............	X.XXX	X.XXX	X.XXX	X.XXX

    Operating Leases:

    Description of Lease Arrangements: _____

    _____

    Future Projected Receipts:

Fiscal Year	Asset Category (1)	(2)	(3)	Totals
Year 1	XXX	XXX	XXX	XXX
Year 2	XXX	XXX	XXX	XXX
Year 3	XXX	XXX	XXX	XXX
Year 4	XXX	XXX	XXX	XXX
Year 5	XXX	XXX	XXX	XXX
After 5 Years	XXX	XXX	XXX	XXX
Total Future Operating Lease Receivables......................	X.XXX	X.XXX	X.XXX	X.XXX

C. **Other Information:** _____

_____

Instructions. SFFAS Nos. 5 and 6 provide the criteria for liability and asset recognition with respect to capital leases.

A.   **Entity as Lessee.**

    Summary of Assets Under Capital Lease: Enter the gross assets under capital lease, by major asset category, and the related total accumulated amortization.

    Description of Lease Arrangements: Provide information that discloses the agency's funding commitments including, but not limited to, the major asset categories and associated lease terms, including renewal options, escalation clauses, contingent rentals restrictions imposed by lease agreements, and the amortization period.

Future Payments Due: Enter future lease payments, by major asset category, for all noncancellable leases with terms longer than one year.

For capital leases, show deductions for imputed interest and executory costs. Separately disclose the portions of the capital lease liability covered by budgetary resources and not covered by budgetary resources (see Appendix B of OMB Circular No. A-11 for additional guidance but observe a difference in terminology: that the term Acapital leases@ as used in this note includes Acapital leases and Alease purchases@ as the terms are used in OMB Circular No. A-11). According to the OMB Circular No. A-11, capital leases entered into during FY 1992 and thereafter are required to be fully funded in the first year of the lease.

B. **Entity as Lessor.**
Description of Lease Arrangements: Provide the information necessary to disclose the commitment of the entity's assets including but not limited to the major asset category and lease terms.

Future Projected Receipts: Enter future lease revenues, by major asset category, for all noncancellable leases with terms longer than one year.

C. **Other Information.** Provide other information necessary for understanding leases that is not disclosed in the above categories.

APPENDIX NO. 7: ACCOUNTING FOR A CAPITAL LEASE BY A LESSEE

Accounting for a Capital Lease by a Lessee

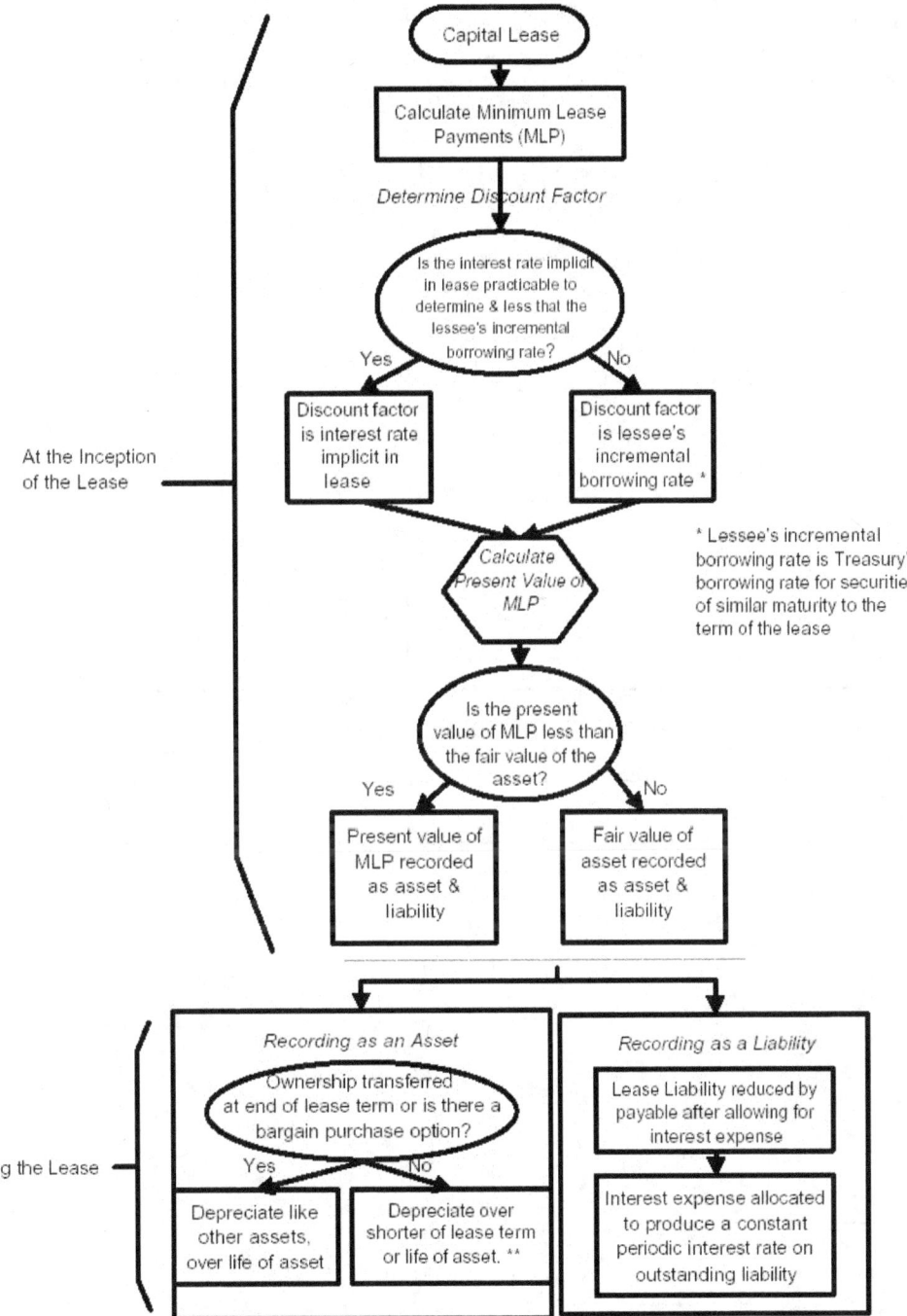

** FASB depreciates over lease term. IFAC depreciates asset over shorter of lease term or useful life.

APPENDIX 8: ILLUSTRATIVE CAPITAL LEASE SCENARIO

Capital Lease Scenario

Assume lease transactions are done in a multi year appropriated fund. The budgetary entries for capital leases are illustrated using the current OMB guidance which requires up front budgetary resources to cover the present value of the lease payments (see OMB circular A11, appendix B).

Equipment A with the useful life of 6 years was leased for 5 years. Assume there is no cancellation clause, executory costs, or property tax involved with the lease. Treasury interest rate is 10.0%. Lease payments including interest are paid in the beginning of the year. Fair market value of the equipment is $120,000. The lease term met the economic life criteria of the capital lease, therefore, the depreciation will be calculated using the lease term[1].

1. Transfer or ownership   NO
2. Bargain purchase option   NO
3. Lease term is greater than or equal to 75%   YES
4. Present value of the lease payment is greater than or equal to 90% FMV of the property   NO

Year	Annual lease payment	Interest on the unpaid lease liability (10%)	Reduction of lease liability	Lease liability
				100,000
1	23,982	0	23,982	76,018
2	23,982	7,602	16,380	59,638
3	23,982	5,964	18,018	41,620
4	23,982	4,162	19,820	21,800
5	23,982	2,182	21,800	0

---

[1] The depreciation period used to calculate depreciation expense depends on which of the capital lease criteria was used to qualify the capital lease. If the lease qualified met ownership transfer or bargain purchase option, the estimated useful life of the asset should be used. If the lease is qualified under economic life or investment recovery, and the lease term is shorter than the estimated useful life of the asset, then the lease term should be used for depreciation purpose.

Capital Lease Scenario

1. To record a simultaneous enactment of appropriations and receipt of warrants.

YEAR 1		
Budgetary Entry		TC
DR 4119 Other Appropriations Realized	107,602	A104
CR 4450 Unapportioned Authority	107,602	
Proprietary Entry		
DR 1010 Fund Balance with Treasury	107,602	
CR 3101 Unexpended Appropriations – Appr. Received	107,602	

2. To record budgetary authority apportioned by OMB and available for allotment.

YEAR 1		
Budgetary Entry		TC
DR 4450 Unapportioned Authority	107,602	A116
CR 4510 Apportionments	107,602	

3. To record allotment of authority.

YEAR 1		
Budgetary Entry		TC
DR 4510 Apportionments	107,602	A120
CR 4610 Allotments – Realized Resources	107,602	

4. A lease contract was signed.

YEAR 1		
Budgetary Entry		TC
DR 4610 Allotments – Realized Resources	100,000	B204
CR 4801 Undelivered Orders Obligations – Unpaid	100,000	

5. The agency acquired the equipment with a lease term of 5 years.

YEAR 1		
Budgetary Entry		TC
DR 4801 Undelivered Orders Obligations – Unpaid	100,000	B302
CR 4901 Delivered Orders Obligations – Unpaid	100,000	
Proprietary Entry		
DR 1810 Assets Under Capital Lease	100,000	B346
CR 2940 Capital Lease Liability	100,000	
DR 3107 Unexpended Appropriations Used	100,000	B134
CR 5700 Expended Appropriations	100,000	

6. To record lease payment.

YEAR 1		
Budgetary Entry		TC
DR 4901 Delivered Orders Obligations – Unpaid	23,982	B110
CR 4902 Delivered Orders Obligations – Paid	23,982	
Proprietary Entry		
DR 2940 Capital Lease Liability	23,982	
CR 1010 Fund Balance with Treasury	23,982	

7. Assume straight line depreciation method is used.

YEAR 1		
Proprietary Entry		TC
DR 6710 Depreciation Expense	20,000	D514
CR 1819 Acc. Depr. For Capital Lease	20,000	

8. To record accrued interest at the end of the year.

YEAR 1		
Budgetary Entry		TC
DR 4610 Allotment – Realized Resources	7,602	B322
CR 4901 Delivered Orders- Obligations. Unpaid.	7,602	
Proprietary Entry		
DR 6330 Other Interest Expense	7,602	
CR 2140 Accrued Interest Payable	7,602	
DR 3107 Unexpended Appropriations Used	7,602	B134
CR 5700 Expended Appropriations	7,602	

Pre - Closing Trial Balance
YEAR 1

YEAR 1	Debit	Credit
Budgetary		
4119	107,602	
4901		83,620
4902	0	23,982
Total	107,602	107,602
Proprietary		
1010	83,620	
1810	100,000	
1819		20,000
2140		7,602
2940		76,018
3101		107,602
3107	107,602	
5700		107,602
6330	7,602	
6710	20,000	
Total	318,824	318,824

Closing Entry

1. To record the closing of revenue, expense and other financing source accounts to cumulative results of operations.

Budgetary Entry		
None		
Proprietary Entry		TC
DR 3310 Cumulative Results of Operations	27,602	F228
CR 6330 Other Interest Expense	7,602	
CR 6710 Depreciation Expense	20,000	
DR 5700 Expended Appropriations	107,602	
CR 3310 Cumulative Results of Operations	107,602	

2. To record the consolidation of actual net-funded resources and reductions for withdrawn funds.

Budgetary Entry		TC
DR 4201 Total Actual Resources Collected	107,602	F204
CR 4119 Other Appropriations Realized	107,602	

3. To record the closing of Expended Authority - Paid.

Budgetary Entry		TC
DR 4902 Delivered Orders – Obligations, Paid	23,982	F214
CR 4201 Total Actual Resources Collected	23,982	

4. To record the closing of fiscal year activity that increases unexpended appropriations.

		TC
Budgetary Entry		
None		
Proprietary Entry		F233
DR 3100 Unexpended Appropriations - Cumulative	107,602	
CR 3107 Unexpended Appropriations - Used	107,602	
DR 3101 Unexpended Appropriations – Appr. Received	107,602	
CR 3100 Unexpended Appropriations – Cumulative	107,602	

Post- Closing Trial Balance
YEAR 1

YEAR 1	Debit	Credit
Budgetary		
4201	83,620	
4901	0	83,620
Total	83,620	83,620
Proprietary		
1010	83,620	
1810	100,000	
1819		20,000
2140		7,602
2940		76,018
3310	0	80,000
Total	183,620	183,620

Department/Agency/Reporting Entity
COMBINED STATEMENT OF BUDGETARY RESOURCES /
SF133, REPORT ON BUDGET EXECUTION (YEAR-END)
For the year ended September 30, Year 1
(in dollars/thousands/millions)

BUDGETARY RESOURCES
1. Budget Authority
   A. Appropriations (4119E)   107,602
2. Unobligated Balance
3. Spending authority From Offsetting Collections
4. Recoveries of Prior-Year Obligations
5. Temporarily Not Available
6. Permanently Not Available   0
7. **Total, Budgetary Resources**   **107,602**

STATUS OF BUDGETARY RESOURCES
8. Obligations Incurred, Direct (4902E/ 4901 E-B)   107,602
9. Unobligated Balance (Currently Available)   0
10. Unobligated Balance (Not Available)   0
11. **Total, Status of Budgetary Resources**   **107,602**

RELATIONSHIP OF OBLIGATIONS TO OUTLAYS
12. Obligated Balance, Net as of October 1
13. Obligated Balance Transferred, Net
14. Obligated Balance, Net, End of Period   83,620
15. Outlays
    A. Disbursements (4902E)   23,018
    B. Collections

FMS 2108 Year-end Closing Statement
YEAR 1

Column 5   (1010E)   83,620dr
Column 10 (4901E)   83,620cr
Total   0

63

Department/Agency/Reporting Entity
CONSOLIDATED BALANCE SHEET
As of September 30, Year 1
(in dollars/thousands/millions)

Assets (Note 2)
    Intragovernmental:

1. Fund Balance with Treasury (Note 3) (1010E)	83,620
6. Total Intragovernmental	83,620
13. General Property, Plant & Equipment (net 1810E, 1819E)	80,000
15. Total Assets	163,620

Liabilities (Note 12)

20. Accrued Interest Payable (2140E)	7,602
26. Other Liabilities (Notes 16, 17 and 18) (2940E)	76,018
27. Total Liabilities	83,620

Net Position:

30. Cumulative Results of Operations (3310)	80,000
31. Total Net Position	80,000
32. Total Liabilities and Net Position	163,620

Department/Agency/Reporting Entity
CONSOLIDATED STATEMENT OF NET COST
For the year ended September 30, Year 1
(in dollars/thousands/millions)

Program Costs:
    Program A:

4. Gross Costs with the public (6330, 6710)	27,602
7. Total net cost	27,602
8. Cost not assigned to programs	0
9. Less Earned revenues not attributed to programs	0
10. Net Cost of Operations	27,602

Department/Agency/Reporting Entity
CONSOLIDATED STATEMENT OF CHANGES IN NET POSITION
For the year ended September 30, Year 1
(in dollars/thousands/millions)

	Cumulative Results of Operations	Unexpended Appropriations
1. Beginning Balances		
2. Prior Period Adjustments		
3. Beginning Balances. As Adjusted		
Budgetary Financing Sources:		
4. Appropriations Received (3101E)		107,602
7. Appropriations Used (3107/5700E)	107,602	(107,602)
Other Financing Sources:		
16. Total Financing Sources	107,602	0
17. Net Cost of Operations	(27,602)	0
18. Ending Balances	80,000	0

Department/Agency/Reporting Entity
COMBINED STATEMENT OF FINANCING
For the year ended September 30, Year 1
(in dollars/thousands/millions)

Resources Used to Finance Activities:
Budgetary Resources Obligated

1. Obligations incurred (4902 E / 4901 E)	107,602
5. Net Obligations (1..4)	107,602
11. Total Resources Used to Finance Activities (5+10)	107,602

Resources Used to Finance Items not Part of the Net Cost of Operations

15. Resources that Finance the Acquisition of Assets or Liquidation of Liabilities (1810 E)	(100,000)
17. Total Resources Used to Finance Items Not Part of the Net Cost of Operations (12..16)	(100,000)
18. Total Resources Used to Finance the Net Cost of Operations (11-17)	7,602

Components of the Net Cost of Operations That Will Not Require
Or Generate Resources in the Current Period:

25. Depreciation and Amortization (1819E)	20,000
29. Total Components of the Net Cost of Operations That Will Not Require Or Generate Resources in the Current Period	20,000
30. Net Cost of Operations (18+29)	27,602

BUDGET PROGRAM AND FINANCING (P&F) SCHEDULE PRIOR-YEAR ACTUAL COLUMN FOR YEAR 1 REPORTING

OBLIGATIONS BY PROGRAM ACTIVITY
Total New Obligations
Line 1000 (4902E / 4901E)   107,602
New Budget Authority, (gross)
Line 2200   107,602

NEW BUDGET AUTHORITY (GROSS), DETAIL
Appropriation (definite)
Line 4000 (4119E)   107,602

TOTAL NEW BUDGET AUTHORITY (GROSS)
Line 7000 (4119E)   107,602
Total new obligations
Line 7310   107,602

CHANGE IN UNPAID OBLIGATIONS
Total Outlays (gross)
Line 7320 (4902E)   (23,982)

OUTLAYS (GROSS), DETAIL
Outlays from new discretionary authority
Line 8690 (4902E)   (23,982)
Total Outlays
Line 8700   (23,982)

NET BUDGET AUTHORITY AND OUTLAYS
Budget Authority (net) (+)
Line 8900   107,602
Outlays (net) (+)
Line 9000   (23,982)

APPENDIX NO. 9: ILLUSTRATIVE SCENARIO FOR OPERATING LEASE WITH A CANCELLATION CLAUSE

Operating Lease With Non-Federal Entity - With a cancellation clause

1. To record funding. The lessee agency signs a 3 year lease agreement on equipment. Yearly rent payment will be $10,000 and the penalty for cancellation is $5,000. **(with a cancellation clause)**

YEAR 1			
Budgetary Entry			TC
DR 4119 Other Appropriations Realized	15,000		A104
CR 4450 Unapportioned Authority		15,000	
Proprietary Entry			
DR 1010 Fund Balance with Treasury	15,000		
CR 3101 Unexpended Appropriations – Appr. Received		15,000	

2. To record budgetary authority apportioned by OMB and available for allotment.

YEAR 1			
Budgetary Entry			TC
DR 4450 Unapportioned Authority	15,000		A116
CR 4510 Apportionments		15,000	

3. To record allotment of authority.

YEAR 1			
Budgetary Entry			TC
DR 4510 Apportionments	15,000		A120
CR 4610 Allotments – Realized Resources		15,000	

4. A lease contract was signed.

YEAR 1			
Budgetary Entry			TC
DR 4610 Allotments – Realized Resources	15,000		B204
CR 4801 Undelivered Orders Obligations – Unpaid		15,000	

5. To make the annual rent payment.

YEAR 1			
Budgetary Entry			TC
DR 4801 Undelivered Orders Obligations – Unpaid	10,000		B302
CR 4902 Delivered Orders Obligations –Paid		10,000	B110
Proprietary Entry			
DR 6100 Operating Expense	10,000		B302
CR 1010 Fund Balance With Treasury		10,000	B110
DR 3107 Unexpended Appropriations Used	10,000		B134
CR 5700 Expended Appropriations		10,000	

Operating Lease With Non-Federal Entity - With a cancellation clause

Pre - Closing Trial Balance
YEAR 1

YEAR 1	Debit	Credit
Budgetary		
4119	15,000	
4801		5,000
4902	0	10,000
Total	15,000	15,000
Proprietary		
1010	5,000	
3301		15,000
5700	10,000	
5700		10,000
6100	10,000	0
Total	25,000	25,000

Closing Entry

1. To record the closing of revenue, expense and other financing source accounts to cumulative results of operations.

		TC
Budgetary Entry		
None		
Proprietary Entry		F228
DR 3310 Cumulative Results of Operations	10,000	
CR 6100 Operating Expense	10,000	
DR 5700 Expended Appropriations	10,000	
CR 3310 Cumulative Results of Operations	10,000	

2. To record the consolidation of actual net-funded resources and reductions for withdrawn funds.

		TC
Budgetary Entry		
DR 4201 Total Actual Resources Collected	15,000	F204
CR 4119 Other Appropriations Realized	15,000	

3. To record the closing of Expended Authority - Paid.

		TC
Budgetary Entry		
DR 4902 Delivered Orders – Obligations, Paid	10,000	F214
CR 4201 Total Actual Resources Collected	10,000	

4. To record the closing of fiscal year activity that increases unexpended appropriations.

Budgetary Entry		TC
None		
Proprietary Entry		F233
DR 3100 Unexpended Appropriations – Cumulative	10,000	
CR 3107 Unexpended Appropriations Used	10,000	
DR 3101 Unexpended Appropriations – Appr. Received	15,000	
CR 3100 Unexpended Appropriations – Cumulative	15,000	

Post- Closing Trial Balance
YEAR 1

YEAR 1	Debit	Credit
Budgetary		
4201	5,000	
4801	0	5,000
Total	5,000	5,000
Proprietary		
1010	5,000	
3100	0	5,000
Total	5,000	5,000

70

Department/Agency/Reporting Entity
COMBINED STATEMENT OF BUDGETARY RESOURCES
SF133, REPORT ON BUDGET EXECUTION (YEAR-END)
For the year ended September 30, Year 1
(in dollars/thousands/millions)

BUDGETARY RESOURCES

1. Budget Authority
   A. Appropriations (4119E)   15,000
2. Unobligated Balance
3. Spending authority From Offsetting Collections
4. Recoveries of Prior-Year Obligations
5. Temporarily Not Available
6. Permanently Not Available   0
7. **Total, Budgetary Resources**   15,000

STATUS OF BUDGETARY RESOURCES

8. Obligations Incurred, Direct (4902E/4801E)   15,000
9. Unobligated Balance (Currently Available)   0
10. Unobligated Balance (Not Available)   0
11. **Total, Status of Budgetary Resources**   15,000

RELATIONSHIP OF OBLIGATIONS TO OUTLAYS

12. Obligated Balance, Net as of October 1
13. Obligated Balance Transferred, Net
14. Obligated Balance, Net, End of Period (4801)   5,000
15. Outlays
    A. Disbursements (4902E)   10,000
    B. Collections

FMS 2108 Year-end Closing Statement
YEAR 1

Column 5   (1010E)   5,000dr
Column 9   (4801E)   5,000cr
Total   0

Department/Agency/Reporting Entity
CONSOLIDATED BALANCE SHEET
As of September 30, Year 1
(in dollars/thousands/millions)

Assets (Note 2)
    Intragovernmental:
    Fund Balance with Treasury (Note 3) (1010)   5,000
    6. Total Intragovernmental   5,000

15. Total Assets   5,000

Liabilities (Note 12)

    27. Total Liabilities   0

Net Position:
    29. Unexpended Appropriations (3100)   5,000
    31. Total Net Position   5,000

32. Total Liabilities and Net Position   5,000

Department/Agency/Reporting Entity
CONSOLIDATED STATEMENT OF NET COST
For the year ended September 30, Year 1
(in dollars/thousands/millions)

Program Costs:
    Program A:
        4. Gross Costs with the public (6100)   10,000

        7. Total net cost   10,000
8. Cost not assigned to programs   0
9. Less: Earned revenues not attributed to programs   0
10. Net Cost of Operations   10,000

Department/Agency/Reporting Entity
CONSOLIDATED STATEMENT OF CHANGES IN NET POSITION
For the year ended September 30, Year 1
(in dollars/thousands/millions)

	Cumulative Results of Operations	Unexpended Appropriations
1. Beginning Balances		
2. Prior Period Adjustments		
3. Beginning Balances, As Adjusted		
Budgetary Financing Sources:		
4. Appropriations Received (3101E)		15,000
7. Appropriations Used (3107/5700E)	10,000	(10,000)
Other Financing Sources:		
16. Total Financing Sources	0	0
17. Net Cost of Operations	(10,000)	0
18. Ending Balances	0	5,000

Department/Agency/Reporting Entity
COMBINED STATEMENT OF FINANCING
For the year ended September 30, Year 1
(in dollars/thousands/millions)

Resources Used to Finance Activities:
Budgetary Resources Obligated

1.	Obligations incurred (4902 E/ 4801 E)	15,000
3.	Obligations Net of Offsetting Collections and Recoveries	15,000
5.	Net Obligations (1..4)	15,000
11.	Total Resources Used to Finance Activities (5+10)	15,000

Resources Used to Finance Items not Part of the Net Cost of Operations

12. Change in Budgetary Resources Obligated for
Goods, Services, and Benefits Ordered but not yet
Provided. (4801)   5,000
17. Total Resources Used to Finance Items
Not Part of the Net Cost of Operations (12..16)   5,000
18. Total Resources Used to Finance the
Net Cost of Operations (11-17)   10,000

Components of the Net Cost of Operations That Will Not Require
Or Generate Resources in the Current Period:

29. Total Components of the Net Cost of Operations
That Will Not Require Or Generate Resources in
the Current Period   0

30. Net Cost of Operations (18+29)   **10,000**

BUDGET PROGRAM AND FINANCING (P&F) SCHEDULE PRIOR-YEAR ACTUAL COLUMN FOR YEAR 1 REPORTING

OBLIGATIONS BY PROGRAM ACTIVITY
Total New Obligations
Line 1000 (4801E-B, 4902E)   15,000

NEW BUDGET AUTHORITY (GROSS), DETAIL
Appropriation (definite)
Line 4000 (4119E)   15,000

TOTAL NEW BUDGET AUTHORITY (GROSS)
Line 7000 (4119E)   15,000

CHANGE IN UNPAID OBLIGATIONS
Total Outlays (gross)
Line 7320 (4902E)   10,000

APPENDIX NO. 10: CLASSIFYING LEASES INVOLVING REAL ESTATE

(1) Leases involving only land are classified in the following manner:

Leases Involving Only Land						
Meets Criterion to Transfer Ownership	Meets Bargain Purchase Option Criterion	Meets One of Two Criterion [82]	Fair Value is Different from Carrying Amount	Meets Two Additional Criteria [83]	Lessee's Lease	Lessor's Lease
		Yes			Capital	
		No			Operating	
Yes			Yes			Sales Type
Yes			No	Yes		Direct Financing or Leveraged
	Yes			Yes		Direct Financing, Leveraged, or Operating
				No		Operating

(2) Leases involving land and building(s) are classified in the following manner:

Leases Involving Land and Building(s)					
Meets Criterion to Transfer Ownership	Meets Bargain Purchase Option Criterion	Meets One of Two Criterion	Fair Value is Different from Carrying Amount	Meets Two Additional Criteria	Accounting
		Yes			Lessee: Land & building are separately capitalized. Present value of minimum lease payments (less executory costs) is allocated between land & building in proportion to their fair values at lease inception. Building is amortized.
Yes			Yes		Lessor: Sales-type lease. Account for lease as a single unit.
Yes			No	Yes	Lessor: Direct financing or leveraged lease.
Yes			No	No	Lessor: Operating lease.
	Yes		Yes		Lessor: Operating lease.
	Yes		No	Yes	Lessor: Direct financing or leveraged lease.
	Yes		No	No	Lessor: Operating lease.
If the lease meets neither the criteria for ownership transfer or bargain purchase option:					
Fair Value of Land is Less than 25% of Total Fair Value	Meets Estimated Economic Life or Fair Value Criteria	Meets Two Additional Criteria	Accounting		
Yes [84]	Yes		Lessee: Capital lease.		
Yes	No		Lessee: Operating lease.		
Yes	Yes	Yes	Lessor: Direct financing, leveraged, or operating lease.		

[82] If lease meets transfer of lease ownership criterion or criterion that the lease contains a bargain purchase option. If answer is no, the lease is an operating lease.

[83] Both criteria must be met: (1) Collectibility of the minimum lease payments is reasonably predictable. (2) No important uncertainties surround the amount of unreimbursable costs yet to be incurred by the lessor under the lease.

[84] Both the lessee and the lessor must consider the land and the building as a single unit for purposes of applying the classification criteria. The estimated economic life of the building is to be used as the estimated economic life of the unit.

Yes	No		Lessor: Operating lease.
Yes		No	Lessor: Operating lease.
No [85]	Building - Yes		Lessee: Building is capital lease. Land is operating lease.
No	Building - No		Lessee: Building and land - operating lease.
No	Building - Yes	Building - Yes	Lessor: Building is direct financing, leveraged or operating lease. Land is operating lease.
No	Building - No		Lessor: Building and land - operating lease.
No		Building - No	Lessor: Building and land - operating lease.

(3) When a lease involves equipment and real estate, the portion of the minimum lease payments associated with the equipment is estimated and considered separately when applying the classification criteria. Real estate and the equipment are accounted for separately by both the lessee and the lessor.

(4) Leases involving only part of a building should be classified like leases involving and land and building(s) if the cost (or carrying amount) and fair value can be objectively determined. If not, the lessor should account for the lease as an operating lease, and the lessee should evaluate the lease by applying the estimated economic life criterion. If that criterion is met, using the estimated economic life of the building in which the leased premise is located, the leased property should be capitalized and accounted for as a capital lease.

---

[85] If the fair value of the land is 25 percent or more of the total fair value of the leased property at the inception of the lease, both the lessee and lessor shall consider the land and the building separately for purposes of applying the classification criteria. The minimum lease payments after deducting executory costs, applicable to the land and the building shall be separated both by the lessee and the lessor by determining the fair value of the land and applying the lessee's incremental borrowing rate to it to determine the annual minimum lease payments applicable to the land element. The remaining minimum lease payments shall be attributed to the building.

APPENDIX NO. 11: FLOW DIAGRAM OF A PUBLIC/ PRIVATE VENTURE

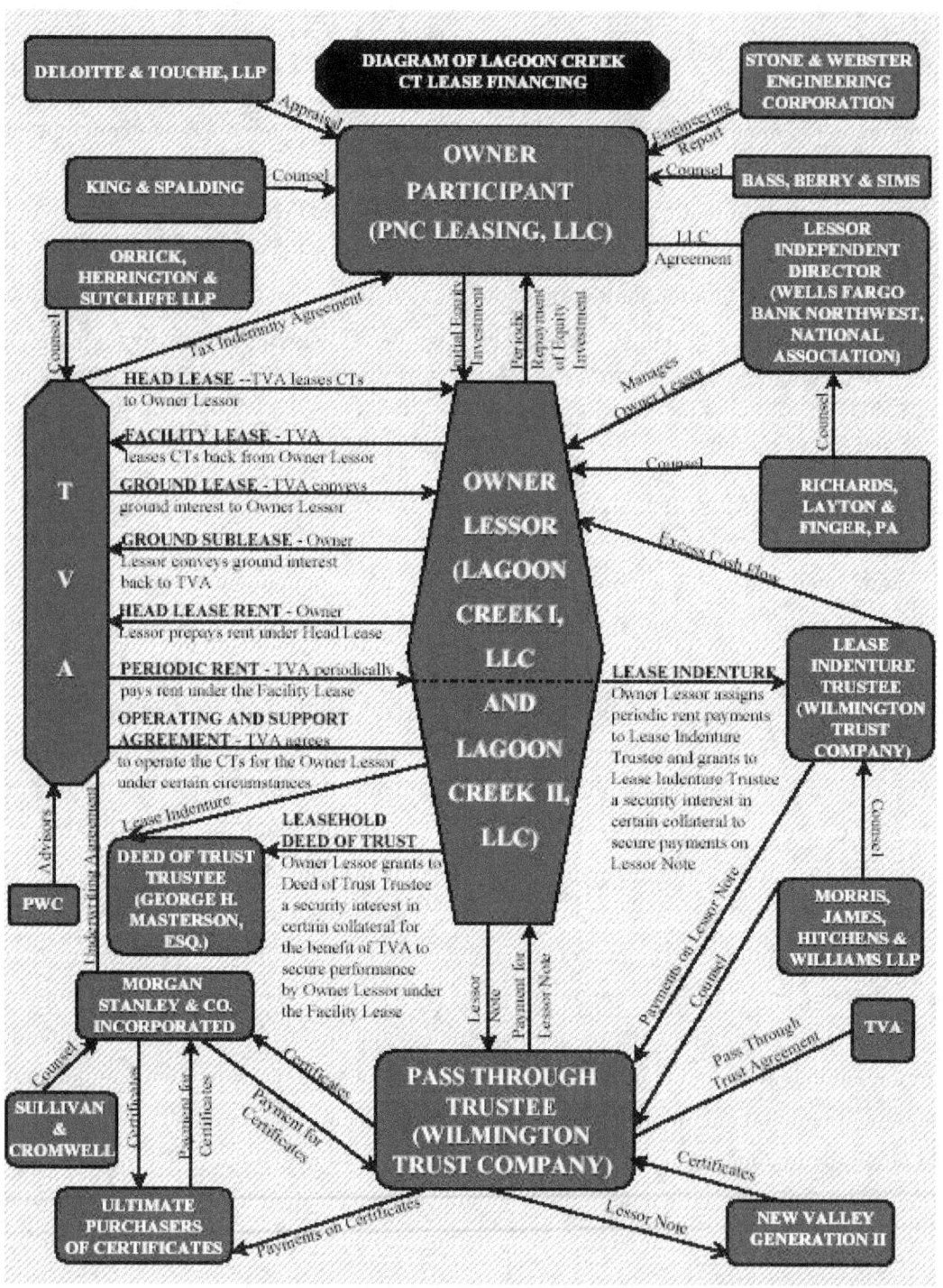

APPENDIX NO. 12: ISSUES - DEPARTMENT OF JUSTICE, OFFICE OF INSPECTOR GENERAL

1. Do occupancy agreements between GSA and federal agencies constitute leases and should these be included in the footnote disclosure for leases?

Justice IG Position: We believe all the agreements between the Department and GSA constitute leases and should be included in the lease disclosure.

Comments: On GSA's website on occupancy agreements, http://hydra.gsa.gov/pbs/pt/opm/pricing_desk/pricing_guide_2k2_2.htm, GSA states that "The OA is not a lease. . ." However, inasmuch as a lease is defined as an agreement conveying the right to use property, plant, and equipment, usually for a stated period of time, it would seem that the occupancy agreements between GSA and Federal agencies are lease agreements since they convey to another agency the right to use space for a set period of time. [86] Contrary to the website statement on occupancy agreements, GSA's *2002 Annual Performance and Accountability Report* states in their disclosure on Property and Equipment, "Substantially, all land, buildings, and leasehold improvements are *leased* (emphasis added) to other Federal agencies under short-term cancelable agreements." [87]

In the case of space that GSA has leased from another entity and subsequently re-leased to a customer Federal agency, the arrangement would be considered a sublease. GSA's Annual Report also states, "Substantially all leased space maintained by the federal Buildings Fund is *sublet* to other Federal agencies at rent charges based upon approximate commercial rates for comparable space. The agreements covering the *sublease arrangements* allow customer agencies, among other things, to terminate the *sublease* at any time. . ." [88] (emphasis added). While FASAB does not discuss subleases or how to account for subleases, FASB does provide guidance to account for and report on subleases and similar transactions. Three specific leasing transactions are described. [89]

1. The leased property is re-leased by the original lessee to a third party, and the lease agreement between the two original parties remains in effect (a sublease).

2. A new lessee is substituted under the original lease agreement. The new lessee becomes the primary obligor under the agreement, and the original lessee may or may not be secondarily liable.

3. A new lessee is substituted through a new agreement, with cancellation of the original lease agreement.

---

[86] An abstract from FASB's Emerging Issues Task Force, EITF 01-8, "Determining Whether an Arrangement is a Lease" states it was generally agreed by the Working Group that "when property, plant, or equipment is explicitly identified and the benefits of the property, plant, or equipment are conveyed based on the passage of time, the arrangement is likely a lease."

[87] GSA, Creating a Successful Future at GSA - 2002 Annual Performance and Accountability Report, page 113.

[88] Ibid. page 16.

[89] SFAS 13, ¶35-40.

Most of GSA occupancy agreements with other agencies would fit the FASB description of a sublease.

Proposed Recommendation: Occupancy agreements between GSA and other Federal agencies should be accounted for, and reported as leases, with appropriate footnote disclosure.

2. Should the footnote disclosure include agreements between the agency and GSA for government-owned buildings? If so, what amount would an entity report for future payments beyond five years when it is expected that the entity is going to occupy the building on a permanent basis?

Justice IG Position: We believe the disclosure should include the agreements with GSA for government-owned buildings. With regards to the amount required to be disclosed for periods after five years, the agency should not include an amount. They should however disclose in a narrative statement the current annual payment and expectation that this payment will continue into future periods.

Comments: Accounting and reporting on occupancy agreements would be the same for the lessee agency, whether or not the property was owned by GSA, or leased by GSA and then subleased to the Federal agency.

Proposed Recommendation: Agreements between the agency and GSA for government-owned buildings should be disclosed in a footnote. It would be acceptable to disclose in a narrative statement the current annual payment and expectation that this payment would continue in the future.

3. Does the accounting treatment differ for GSA- or government-owned buildings versus GSA leased buildings?

Justice IG Position: No

Comments: From the Federal agency lessee's perspective, the accounting treatment would not differ for a GSA- or government-owned building versus a GSA-leased building.

Proposed Recommendation: See Issue No. 2 above.

4. What is the proper accounting treatment for leasehold improvements by Federal agencies? When would leasehold improvements be capitalized or expensed? What is considered an improvement?

Justice IG Position: We believe a leasehold improvement should be capitalized if the expenditures for the improvement: 1) expand the capacity of an asset or otherwise upgrade it to serve needs different from, or significantly greater than, those originally intended; 2) exceed the capitalization threshold ($100,000 for DOJ); and 3) benefit more than one accounting period. Further these leasehold improvements should be amortized by the lessee (or the party using the asset) and included in the Federal agency's property, plant, and equipment. In addition, our interpretation of SFFAS No. 6 is that all capitalizable leasehold improvements are to be included in property, plant, and equipment, not just those leasehold improvements to property being leased through a capital lease.

Comments: Limited guidance is given by FASAB on accounting for specifically leasehold improvements. SFFAS No. 6, paragraph 18 states that PP&E includes assets acquired through capital leases, *including leasehold improvements*, and paragraph 37, with respect to expense recognition and general PP&E, states,

> Costs which either extend the useful life of an existing general PP&E, or enlarge or improve its capacity shall be capitalized and depreciated/amortized over the remaining useful life of the associated general PP&E.

Proposed Recommendation: The cost of leasehold improvements should be depreciated over either the shorter of the life of the improvement or the remaining lease term. Generally, nonrecurring capital expenditures, over certain thresholds, that add to the service potential of the asset should be capitalized and allocated to future revenue, and expenditures to maintain the asset in good operating condition are recognized as expenses.

5. Is a bona-fide lease agreement necessary for improvements to be capitalized or, more specifically, should improvements made to property occupied via an occupancy agreement also be capitalized?

Justice IG Position: No, a bona-fide lease agreement is not necessary for leasehold improvements to be capitalized. We believe that improvements made to property occupied via an occupancy agreement should be capitalized. The definition of a lease states that a lease includes agreements that convey the right to use property for a specified period, and we believe occupancy agreements fit this definition.

Comments: Yes, the cost of improvements made to property leased under an occupancy agreement should be capitalized. The question is whether GSA or the Federal agency should capitalize the costs. When GSA pays for the improvement costs, they capitalize the costs (over certain thresholds) and the Federal agency is charged a higher rent. The Federal agency, in turn, should expense these costs. If the Federal agency pays for the improvement costs, they should capitalize the improvement costs and depreciate them over either the period of occupancy or the life of the improvement, whichever is shorter. GSA would treat these costs as an expense.

Proposed Recommendation: The cost of improvements not paid by GSA, and over the agency's thresholds, should be capitalized and amortized by the Federal agency.

6. Can further clarification or examples be provided on what is a leasehold improvement versus what is maintenance?

Justice IG Position: Professional judgment should be exercised on a case-by-case basis. The dollar amount of the expenditure and the threshold for capitalization should be considered in any decision. The Federal GAAP definition of maintenance is "the act of keeping fixed assets in usable condition. It includes preventive maintenance, normal repairs, replacement of part and structural components, and other activities needed to preserve the asset so that it continues to provide acceptable services and achieves its expected life. Maintenance excludes activities aimed at expanding the capacity of an asset or otherwise upgrading it to serve needs different from, or significantly greater than, those originally intended."

Comments: Agree with Justice IG.

Proposed Recommendation: Agree with Justice IG.

7. If leasehold improvements are funded through higher rent payments rather than a one-time payment by the lessee, does this change the accounting treatment for leasehold improvements?

Justice IG Position: No. We do not believe that leasehold improvements that are funded through higher rent payments rather than a one-time payment by the lessee change the accounting treatment for those leasehold improvements. The leasehold improvements in both situations should be capitalized and amortized over time.

Comments: GSA has stated that if the Federal agency is being charged a higher rent to recover the cost of the improvement, GSA has capitalized and amortized the improvement costs. It would be inappropriate for the Federal agency to capitalize and amortize the same costs.

Proposed Recommendation: When GSA capitalizes and amortizes the improvement costs presumably to ready the building for occupancy, then passes on the costs to the agency in the form of a higher rent, the agency should expense these costs.

8. Does this accounting treatment for capitalization change if an occupancy agreement specifically provides cancelable or non-cancelable clauses based on availability of funding?

Justice IG Position: No. We believe that the fiscal funding clause contained in occupancy agreements does not effect the accounting treatment. Further we believe a contingency clause on future funding does not make the lease cancelable in accordance with the private sector GAAP guidelines. We believe that these types of leases should be considered non-cancelable. Given that, we believe that improvements made under non-cancelable leases should be capitalized.

Comments: There seems to be several issues here: 1) What are the cancellation clauses included in the GSA occupancy agreements; do they include a fiscal funding clause, 2) Does the existence of a fiscal funding clause affect the accounting treatment of a leasehold improvement, 3) If the occupancy agreement is an operating lease, can the leasehold improvement be capitalized and amortized?

According to GSA, in most cases, agencies are able to cancel the agreements with 120-day notice and there is not a fiscal funding clause. There are a few agreements that are not cancelable because GSA has built the facility to the agency's specific requirements. For example, laboratories built to the unique requirements of the Drug Enforcement Agency are covered in 10-year, non-cancelable agreements.

Proposed Recommendation: Leases with a cancellation clause are generally considered operating leases. With respect to a fiscal funding clause, FASB guidance [90] states that an assessment must be made to determine the likelihood of the lease being canceled due to a lack of funding. If the likelihood of cancellation is remote, the lease agreement should be considered a non-cancelable lease; if not, the lease is considered cancelable, and an operating lease. Generally, the likelihood of a government lessee terminating the lease due to a lack of funds is remote. [91] With respect to capitalizing the leasehold improvement, we agree with Justice IG that the improvement should be capitalized.

9. How do the cancellation and funding clauses affect the accounting and disclosure aspects of these transactions?

Comments: See question 8. for discussion on cancellation and funding clauses.

Proposed Recommendation: Leases with a cancellation clause are generally considered operating leases and should be accounted for, and disclosed, accordingly. Leases that are non-cancelable, may be classified as a capital lease if the lease meets one of the four classification criteria.

---

[90] SFFAS 13, ¶ 5(f), FTB79-10, <u>Fiscal Funding Clauses in Lease Agreements</u>.
[91] NCGAS 5, ¶ 18-21.

APPENDIX NO. 13: EXCERPTS ON LEASES FROM SFFAS NO. 5 ACCOUNTING FOR LIABILITIES OF THE FEDERAL GOVERNMENT

Capital leases -- In a lease transaction, the lessee should report a liability when one or more of four specified capital lease criteria are met (see detailed criteria below). The amount to be recorded by the lessee as a liability[92] under a capital lease is the present value of the rental and other minimum lease payments during the lease term, excluding that portion of the payments representing executory cost to be paid by the lessor.

43   **Capital leases** are leases that transfer substantially all the benefits and risks of ownership to the lessee. If, at its inception, a lease meets one or more of the following four criteria, the lease should be classified as a capital lease by the lessee:

- The lease transfers ownership of the property to the lessee by the end of the lease term.

- The lease contains an option to purchase the leased property at a bargain price.

- The lease term is equal to or greater than 75 percent of the estimated economic life of the leased property.

- The present value of rental and other minimum lease payments, excluding that portion of the payments representing executory cost, equals or exceeds 90 percent of the fair value of the leased property.

The last two criteria are not applicable when the beginning of the lease term falls within the last 25 percent of the total estimated economic life of the leased property. If a lease does not meet at least one of the above criteria it should be classified as an operating lease.

44   The amount to be recorded by the lessee as a liability under a capital lease is the present value of the rental and other minimum lease payments during the lease term, excluding that portion of the payments representing executory cost to be paid by the lessor.[93] However, if the amount so determined exceeds the fair value of the leased property at the inception of the lease, the amount recorded as the liability should be the fair value. If the portion of the minimum lease payments representing executory cost is not determinable from the lease provisions, the amount should be estimated.

45   The discount rate to be used in determining the present value of the minimum lease payments ordinarily would be the lessee's incremental borrowing rate unless (1) it is practicable for the lessee to learn the implicit rate computed by the lessor and (2) the implicit rate computed by the lessor is less than the lessee's incremental borrowing rate. If both these conditions are met, the lessee shall use the implicit rate. The lessee's incremental borrowing rate shall be the Treasury borrowing rate for securities of similar maturity to the term of the lease.

---

[92]"The cost of general property, plant, and equipment acquired under a capital lease shall be equal to the amount recognized as a liability for the capital lease at its inception." (See SFFAS No. 6, *Property, Plant, and Equipment*.)

[93]"The cost of general property, plant, and equipment acquired under a capital lease shall be equal to the amount recognized as a liability for the capital lease at its inception. See SFFAS No. 6, *Accounting for Property, Plant, and Equipment*.

46   During the lease term, each minimum lease payment should be allocated between a reduction of the obligation and interest expense so as to produce a constant periodic rate of interest on the remaining balance of the liability.[94]

---

[94]OMB Circular No. A-11, "Preparation and Submission of Annual Budget Estimates," explains the measurement of budget authority, outlays, and debt for the budget in the case of lease-purchases and other capital leases. Circular A-94, "Guidelines and Discount Rates for Benefit-Cost Analysis of Federal Programs," provides the requirements under which a lease-purchase or other capital lease has to be justified and the analytical methods that need to be followed.

APPENDIX NO. 14: EXCERPTS ON LEASES FROM SFFAS NO. 6 ACCOUNTING FOR PROPERTY, PLANT, AND EQUIPMENT

The Federal Government's investment in PP&E exceeds $1 trillion[95] and includes many types of PP&E used for many different purposes. "PP&E" is defined as follows:

> Tangible assets that (1) have an estimated useful life of 2 or more years, (2) are not intended for sale in the ordinary course of business, and (3) are intended to be used or available for use by the entity.

18   Property, plant, and equipment also includes:

- assets acquired through capital leases (See paragraph 0), including leasehold improvements;
- property owned by the reporting entity in the hands of others (e.g., state and local governments, colleges and universities, or Federal contractors); and
- land rights.[96]

20   <u>Capital leases</u> are leases that transfer substantially all the benefits and risks of ownership to the lessee. If, at its inception, a lease meets one or more of the following four criteria,[97] the lease should be classified as a capital lease by the lessee. Otherwise, it should be classified as an operating lease.[98]

- The lease transfers ownership of the property to the lessee by the end of the lease term.
- The lease contains an option to purchase the leased property at a bargain price.
- The lease term is equal to or greater than 75 percent of the estimated economic life[99] of the leased property.
- The present value of rental and other minimum lease payments, excluding that portion of the payments representing executory cost, equals or exceeds 90 percent of the fair value[100] of the leased property.

---

[95] Department of the Treasury, Financial Management Service, *Consolidated Financial Statements of the United States Government*, prototype 1993, p. 23. The prototype statements provide gross historical cost investment amounts for all PP&E recorded by government entities. These amounts have not been audited.

[96] "Land rights" are interests and privileges held by the entity in land owned by others, such as leaseholds, easements, water and water power rights, diversion rights, submersion rights, rights-of-way, and other like interests in land.

[97] Note that the criteria for identifying capital leases for financial reporting purposes differ from OMB criteria for budget scoring of leases. OMB Circular No. A-11, *Preparation and Submission of Budget Estimates*, includes criteria for identifying operating leases in Appendix B. OMB provides four additional criteria which relate to the level of private sector risk involved in a lease-purchase agreement. This is necessary because, for budget purposes, there is a distinction between lease-purchases with more or less risk. This distinction is not made in the financial reports and, therefore, FASAB does not include the four criteria related to risk levels.

[98] "Operating leases" of PP&E are leases in which the Federal entity does not assume the risks of ownership of the PP&E. Multi-year service contracts and multi-year purchase contracts for expendable commodities are not capital leases.

[99] "Estimated economic life of leased property" is the estimated remaining period during which the property is expected to be economically usable by one or more users, with normal repairs and maintenance, for the purpose for which it was intended at the inception of the lease, without limitation by the lease term.

[100] "Fair value" is the price for which an asset could be bought or sold in an arm's-length transaction between unrelated parties (e.g., between a willing buyer and a willing seller). (adapted from <u>Kohler's Dictionary for Accountants</u>)

The last two criteria are not applicable when the beginning of the lease term falls within the last 25 percent of the total estimated economic life of the leased property.

29   The cost of general PP&E acquired under a **capital lease** shall be equal to the amount recognized as a liability for the capital lease at its inception (i.e., the net present value of the lease payments calculated as specified in the liability standard[101] unless the net present value exceeds the fair value of the asset).

---

[101]See Statement of Recommended Accounting Standards No. 5, *Accounting for Liabilities of the Federal Government*.

BIBLIOGRAPY FOR LEASES

Congressional Budget Office, *A CBO Paper – The Budgetary Treatment of Leases and Public/Private Ventures*, February 2003.

Congressional Budget Office, Letter to Senator Don Nickels dated August 26, 2003, *Assessment of the Air Force's Plan to Acquire 100 Boeing Tanker Aircraft*.

Federal Aviation Administration, FY 2002 Performance and Accountability Report.

Financial Management Service, Department of the Treasury, U.S. Government Standard General Ledger Chart of Accounts, June 2003.

Financial Management Service, Department of the Treasury, *Approved Scenarios - Leases*, March 2001.

General Accounting Office, *Public Buildings: Budget Scorekeeping Prompts Difficult Decisions*, GAO/T-AIMD-GGD-94-43, October 28, 1993.

General Accounting Office, *Energy Conservation: Energy Savings Performance Contracting in Federal Agencies*, GAO/RCED-96-215, September 1996.

General Accounting Office, Letter to Representative James A. Traficant, Jr., *Space Acquisition cost: Comparison of GSA Estimates for Three Alternatives,* GAO/GGD-97-148R, August 6, 1997.

General Accounting Office, *Public-Private Partnerships: Key Elements of Federal Building and Facility Partnerships,* GAO/GGD-00-23, February 1999.

General Accounting Office, *General Services Administration: Leasing Practices in Selected Regions,* GAO/GGD-00-88, April 2000.

General Accounting Office, Letter to Senator James M. Inhofe dated June 5, 2001, Acquisition of Leased Space for the U.S. Patent and Trademark Office, GAO-01-578R.

General Accounting Office, *Public-Private Partnerships: Pilot Program Needed to Demonstrate the Actual Benefits of Using Partnerships*, GAO-01-906, July 2001.

General Accounting Office, *Budget Scoring: Budget Scoring Affects Some Lease Terms but Full Extent is Uncertain*, GAO-01-929, August 2001.

General Accounting Office, *Public-Private Partnerships: Factors to Consider When Deliberating Governmental Use as a Real Property Management Tool*, Statement of Bernard L. Ungar, Director, Physical Infrastructure Issues, GAO-02-46T, October 1, 2001.

General Accounting Office, Letter to Senator John McCain dated May 15, 2002, *Air Force Aircraft: Preliminary Information on Air Force Tanker Leasing*, GAO-02-724R.

General Accounting Office, Defense Infrastructure: *Greater Management Emphasis Needed to Increase the Services' Use of Expanded Leasing Authority*, GAO-02-475, June 2002.

General Accounting Office, *Military Housing: Management Improvements Needed as the Pace of Privatization Quickens*, GAO-02-624, June 2002.

General Accounting Office, *Contract Management: Commercial Use of Share-in-Savings Contracting*, GAO-03-327, January 2003.

General Accounting Office, *Tennessee Valley Authority: Information on Lease-Leaseback and Other Financing Arrangements*, GAO-03-784, June 2003.

General Accounting Office, *Military Aircraft: Considerations in Reviewing the Air Force Proposal to Lease Aerial Refueling Aircraft*, Statement of Neal P. Curtin, Director, Defense Capabilities and Management, GAO-03-1048T, July 23, 2003.

General Accounting Office, *Budget Issues: Alternative Approaches to Finance Federal Capital*, GAO-03-1001, August 2003.

General Services Administration, *Creating a Successful Future at GSA: 2002 Annual Performance and Accountability Report*.

McGregor, Warren, *Accounting for Leases: A New Approach, Recognition by Lessees of Assets and Liabilities Arising Under Lease Contracts*, No. 163-A, Financial Accounting Foundation, July 1996.

Mosich, A. N., *Intermediate Accounting*, McGraw-Hill Book Company, Revised Sixth Edition.

Nailor, Hans; Lennard, Andrew; *Leases: Implementation of a New Approach*, No. 206-A, Financial Accounting Foundation, February 2000.

Office of Management and Budget, OMB Circular A-94, *Guidelines and Discount Rates for Benefit-Cost Analysis of Federal Programs*, revised January 22, 2002.

Office of Management and Budget, OMB Bulletin No. 01-09, *Form and Content of Agency Financial Statements*, September 25, 2001.

Office of Management and Budget, OMB Circular A-11, *Preparation, Submission, and Execution of the Budget, Appendix B - Scoring Lease-Purchases and Leases of Capital Assets*, July 25, 2003.

Tierney, Cornelius E., *Federal Accounting Handbook*, John Wiley & Sons, Inc., 200.

Wolk, Harry I., Tearney, Michael G, Dodd, James L., Accounting Theory: A Conceptual and Institutional Approach, South-Western College Publishing, fifth edition, Chapter 17 Leases.

Proposed Legislation:

H.R. 2573, Public Private Partnership Act of 2003

H.R. 2548, Federal Property Asset Management Reform Act of 2003